I0073858

Death of A Website

Don't Make These 7 Killer Website Mistakes

by Dwainia Grey

Copyright @ 2017 Dwainia Grey

All rights reserved. No part of this book may be reproduced, stored, or transmitted in any form or by any means, including scanning, photocopying, recording, or other electronic or mechanical methods, without the prior written permission of the publisher, except in the case of brief quotations embodied in critical reviews and certain other noncommercial uses permitted by copyright law. For permission requests, email info@awesomebizonline.com subject line "Attention Permissions Coordinator"

Limit of liability/disclaimer of warranty: While the publisher and author have used their best efforts in preparing this book they make no representations or warranties with respect to accuracy or completeness of the contents of this document and specifically disclaim any implied warranties of merchantability or fitness for particular purpose. No warranty may be created or extended by sales representatives, promoters, or written sales materials.

The advice and strategies contained herein may not be suitable for your situation. You should consult with a professional where appropriate. Neither the publisher nor author shall be liable for any loss of profit or any other commercial damages, including but not limited to special, incidental, consequential, or other damages.

Permissions
Please feel free to take photos of this book (or your use of it) for the purposes of review or social media sharing. Please do not photograph the whole book.

Published by
GreyChild Communications
Toronto, ON

Social Media Marketing / Dwainia Grey
ISBN-13: 978-0-9951650-7-6

This book is dedicated to all the business owners that want better websites.

Table of Contents

Chapter One
#WebDOA

Death of A Website and How to Avoid It

This book is for all the Empowerpreneurs whose websites are not working for them. Whether or not you have a website this book is for you. If you don't have a website this book can be used as a step by step guide and if you have a website it will show you how to improve your website to increase sales.

Imagine how much better your business and life will be when your website actually produces profits for your business instead of sitting there as an expense on your Profit and Loss statements.

This book is filled with questions to get you thinking about how to make your website more effective as a branding, lead generating and sales tool.

Take your time and complete each section. Use these surveys to go through your website and see where it needs improvement. Get others to take the surveys and review your site.

At the end of each chapter you will see an ACTION PLAN to get you started in making your website better.

- How will you measure success?
- Whom do you envision as your core users?
- What do you want those users to gain by visiting your website?
- What do you want users to do after or while they're on your website?
- How does your idea for a website compare with others?
- Do you expect to make money on your website?

Chapter One
Is Your Website Still There?

If you are reading this book you are not satisfied with your website. Why not? Think about it. What changes would you make and why?

Do you update or maintain your website on a regular basis?

Is your website still there?
This is very valid question.
I went to see a prospective client and he went to show me his website and it wasn't there.
On further investigation the domain hadn't been renewed in two years.
This means he hasn't checked his website in two whole years.
He has this listed on his business card.

- Do you have a website?
- Do you get clients from this website?
- Can your business be found online?

A good website takes some of the workload off your marketing and selling efforts if done properly. An effective website is the face of your brand, directing clients where you need to them to go, providing answers and credibility and convinces them to buy. A good website will align the right clients with the right products and services.

Why do You Need a Website?
The traditional yellow pages have been replaced; the majority of people looking for products and services go online first. Many people will research by checking out the company and service/product offerings on the Internet before they make a decision. They also comparison shop this way.

Here are the top 5 reasons why you need a website now. These do not include the most important - attract new customers.
1. 96% of consumers visit the web to research before they buy.

2. Save time. Provide valuable information online.

3. Your competitor is online. Actually 80% of businesses are online.

4. Be accessible 24/7

5. Branding

In today's world how could you not have a website?

Advertising Tool

Use your website to get more customers, learn to use this tool to generate genuine interest in your products and services effectively.

Customer Service Tool

One often overlooked aspects of a website is the comfort your customers receive from having 24 /7 customer service available to them
By creating a website that is inviting, informative, and easy to navigate through, you are giving your customers (and potential customers) an avenue through which they can keep in regular "contact" with your business. Remember that your brand is an abstract thing, based on the impression you give people, as well as all the things they associate with your business. Forging a connection with your business is integral to strengthening your brand, and a great website is a very

effective way of doing that. Today's consumers are online performing research before purchasing.

Lead Generation Tool
Use your website to turn visitors into buyers and leads. Your website can be a gateway to increase leads and sales, and generate repeat business and referrals.

How to Use This Book

Review each page of your website in each category. Grade each page on the # categories and take notes to begin making improvements. Each section has an action plan that allows you to start making improvements immediately.

Each section is worth 100 points.

Place your totals on this page

Score   **Points**

Design and Branding
Design
Branding
Preferred Client
Your Story
Your Offer
Design and Branding Score

Content
Website Content
Blogging

SEO
Marketing Message
Must Haves
Content Score

Selling
Call To Action
Lead Generation
Services
Products
E-Commerce
Selling Score

Marketing
Get Found
Social Media
Online Reputation Management
Email
Advertising
Marketing Score

Optimization, Maintenance, and Measurement
Speed
Broken Links
Error Page
Maintenance
Metrics
Optimization, Maintenance, and Measurement Score

Take the total score and divide by 5.

Scale
01-25 – Site Needs a Complete Overhaul

26-50 – Site Needs Improvement

51-75 – Focus on improving areas that you scored low on

75-100 – Ask 5 people to score your site and compare results

Please note for each yes or no question yes is equivalent to five (5) and no is equivalent to zero (0).

#

How to Use This Book

Chapter Two
The Motive

The first offence is creating a website without an objective. Establish the motive/objective for your website.

What is your Website Objective?

For your website to succeed you have to know what success is to you. Why do you have a website?

Nice Objectives
- Branding
- Launch a new product
- Expose an existing product
- Provide information

Nice objectives are secondary. They bring focus & purpose to the design of the website. As Empowerpreneurs we must remember we are in a business and our business is to empower others while making money and your website should be making money.

Your objective must be measurable. What is success to you? How do you know if you have achieved it?

Write down your top 3 objectives for your website?

- What do you want to accomplish?
- What do you want (personal)?
- What do you need (professional)?

Does your website, and content align with those objectives? If not, why? What changes do you need to make?
We reviewed nice objectives, your objectives, now let's look at **Real Objectives**.

The reality is - the objective of every website can be summed up into 3 goals for every business.

Attract Visitors - Use online and offline marketing to attract visitors. With the amount of noise and traffic on the web it's no longer a "build it and they will come". Use your website to promote your brand, provide information, increase sales

Capture Qualified Leads - A website is the perfect lead generation tool. Use your website to collect names and addresses to later connect with potential clients.

Turn Leads Into Sales - Convert website visitors into paying customers. Whether your site is e-commerce or not it should be compelling enough for you to capture a lead or for the visitor to want to buy or get more information to close the sale.

Attract Visitors

A money making website should not only attract new visitors but also entice visitors to return. As visitors keep returning to your awesome website you start building trust and are more likely to turn visitors into clients.

Capture Qualified Leads

The next steps are to convert visitors into leads and in turn convert leads into sales.

A money making website attracts qualified leads. These are potential clients that already have interest to buy and the capability to buy. Don't make the mistake of attracting a large amount of leads with an open promotion such as a free iPad. Think quality over quantity and use a promotion that ties into your offering. You can't turn unqualified - people not interested in your products and services into sales.

Convert Leads into Sales
What is a money making website without actual sales? The perfect website will make sales directly where people buy from the website or indirectly where it supports converting leads into sales.

Your website can contain everything your clients could possibly want, but if it's poorly written or structured, they may not realize the information is there.

Look at your website. Does your website currently meet real objectives?

First Impression

"You should be able to tell what the website is about in seconds."

You have a very limited window of time to attract visitors' attention and seize their interest long enough to get them to stay and explore your website. You have 3 seconds (attention span on the web) to capture the attention of a visitor.

When visitors come to your website, they want to know what's in it for me.
1. Where am I?

2. What can I do here?

3. Why should I do it?

When visitors come to your website you don't want them leaving immediately confused. Website first impression is too vital for you not to invest in good design.

What do you want visitors to do? This seems like a simple question but most website owners spend more time worrying about what shade of blue the header is. Review the top retail sites such as Amazon and the top people in your industry. How pretty is too pretty? Do you want people to look at your website and remark what on that awesome shade of blue or do you want them to buy something? Come up with a plan to attract visitors, convert leads, and increase sales.

Start Planning

This book not only helps you improve your website for sales, but it also teaches you how to plan your online marketing with your website at the centre.

Step 1 - Attract Visitors

- Use your website to attract and entice visitors.
- Use design to create functionality.
- Use branding to attract and build recognition.
- Use content to be informative, provide useful, valuable information. Create an awesome blog.
- Use marketing, such as social media to attract visitors.
- Use SEO to get search engines to recommend you.
- Use your website to make sales. It can be a 24/7 ATM that makes you money while you sleep.

Step 2 - Qualified Leads

Use your website to attract not just any lead but qualified leads.

The trick to get qualified leads is to
1. Define and know your client
- Create a clear description of your client
- Create all materials to communicate with your preferred client
- Remove objections by building trust

2. Provide a way to capture leads on your website
- Create awesome offers on your website - attract people that want what you are selling
- Use compelling opt-ins to encourage visitors to signup
- Follow through and deliver

3. Nurture Leads
Now you have a bunch of leads that you have received your offer, what's next? It should not be a cheesy sales pitch. What's next is useful information in a series of newsletters, with a call to action that now targets segments within your target market and unobtrusive offers.

This communication builds trust, credibility and the call to action and offers will get them moving one step closer to making a purchase.

Step 3 - Sales

Your website should be a hub of information on your business, your products and services. If I'm looking for that plumbing gizmo that you sell, I should find it with all the information that will help me decide to buy on your website. What leads me to buy from you is the fact that:

1. I know more about your business,

2. Due to the amount of other information you have provided via your blog and product information etc., I know that you are a professional that likes to help people,

3. I know you have a list of satisfied customers from the testimonials listed

All of this is on your website and makes me want to purchase from you despite the price, and despite the 20% off offered by the competition.

Is your website offering enough information to help your visitors come to a buying decision?

Does your website connect, capture and convert?

Step 4 - Optimize and Maintain

Now that you have a money making website, let's keep it that way.

You have to optimize, update, and maintain your website continually. And once you have created objectives you have to ensure your website is meeting them. Use metrics to track and monitor your website.

Action Plan

Take a moment and complete the action plan for your motive to save your website.

Write down your top 3 nice objectives for your website.

Download and complete the Objective Worksheet in the Death of A Website Death of A Website Workbook and Planner and Planner.

As you read through this book start creating your action plan based on the 4 steps of your Website Planning.

Step 1 - Attract Visitors
Step 2 - Qualified Leads
Step 3 - Sales
Step 4 - Optimize and Maintain

Chapter Three
The Alibi

Strategy

Before you commit the crime, create your alibi. Decide on the backend of your website with the trinity of the domain, hosting and CMS (WordPress) to ensure your website is fully supported.

The 7 Keys to Choosing a Domain

Start your website right with a proper domain name. Choosing the right domain name does not have to be hard. Follow the 7 steps below for choosing the right domain name to reflect you, your brand, and your business.

1. Use your brand or business name whenever possible for brand recognition purposes

2. Be sure it is easy to spell

3. Aim to have at least one keyword in it: marketing, SEO

4. Use .com

5. Be careful with singular and plural: girl versus girls, especially if the pluralized word is next to a word that starts with an s: girlsspace versus girlspace

6. Check your spelling and typing twice.

7. Use your URL on every piece of promotional material you create, from business cards to letterhead to flyers.

Brainstorm using:
- Keywords

- Your business name
- Business initials
- Industry
- Niche

To come up with the URL that is right for you.

Narrow down your list to 3-5 choices
1-

2-

3-

4-

5-

Go to namecheap.com and start checking availability.

Domain names are purchased on an annual basis and can be renewed at the end of the year. If the domain is not renewed, it will be released for purchase. A lot of times it is scooped up by domain resellers and resold at a higher price.

10 Ways to Find the Best Webhosting

There are many affordable web hosting options especially using the ever popular WordPress. Choosing a hosting company/plan comes down to.

1. Specs - what do you need the website to do?
- Is it media heavy with a lot of images and or video?

- Is it an e-commerce website? (Requires SSL)
- Size of website

2. Hosting reliability:
- Uptime
- Speed and performance
- Security
- Reliability

3. Easy to upgrade - As your business grows you may outgrow your hosting plan, you want a provider that makes it easy to upgrade

4. Features - Most companies now provide unlimited domains, and unlimited emails accounts but you should know your limitations.

Other features that most hosting companies include are:
- Database management
- Domain registration
- Subdomains
- SSL
- FTP
- Etc.

5. Cost - Is it competitive and affordable? What is the renewal cost? Don't be fooled by your first year (introductory) price.

6. Control Panel - Most companies provide cPanel to manage the backend of your website which is easy to use to access email, user accounts, files, database, etc. If it's not cPanel, is it easy to use?

7. Read the terms of service (TOS). Under what conditions can you or the company cancel or suspend service?

8. Refund policy. What happens if you cancel during the trial period? Is there a trial period? What about refunds after the trial period?

9. Site backup. What happens if your website crashes or you get hacked? It's rare and you should be backing up on your own, however, does the hosting company provide regular backups? Are you able to manage backups with the control panel? Is there auto backup available and can you restore the website yourself?

10. Lastly, customer service and support. Is there a live chat? How long does it take to answer a support ticket? Is there a phone number to call - what are the hours? What channels are available 24/7 - chat, email, ticket, phone? How friendly and helpful is the support staff? What is their response time for resolving issues?

Why WordPress

Build your website on a Content Management System (CMS) such as WordPress.

Ensure your website is not domain dependent. Your website should be portable and it should be easy to move it to a different web hosting company.

Is your CMS a licensed product?

There are many content management systems out there that are built for blogging, but I recommend WordPress especially if you are just starting out. Why? Because it's easy.

Not only is WordPress one of the easiest platforms to use, but search engines also love it because it's search engine friendly. Here are the top 5 reasons to use WordPress.

1. WordPress is Free. I recommend you use the self-hosted option to own your own domain and content. With the self-hosted option, you only have to pay for your domain and hosting because the WordPress CMS is free to use.

2. WordPress is Customizable. With the use of plugins and themes and a great web designer/developer you make WordPress look however you want and do whatever you want.

3. WordPress is Scalable. You can run a small blog, an e-commerce site or a content publishing empire. The New York Times, CNN, Forbes, Mashable, and many others use WordPress for their sites.

4. WordPress is a Content Management System by definition. It comes with its own built-in scheduler, so you can even schedule blog posts for two or more years if you wanted to. WordPress makes it easy to post, update and edit posts on any computer using any browser. It also allows for multiple users, authors, and editors.

5. WordPress is Media Friendly. You can add video, audio, and images with ease. Also allows for embeds from popular sites such as YouTube.

Research the many options for the best CMS solution for your needs.

Using WordPress

Take time and learn how to use WordPress. If you need more help consider taking my online WordPress course that I also offer in workshops.

Installation

Follow the instruction on how to install WordPress on your website. Configure it for optimal use.

When choosing a premium theme or plugin ensure that it has the capability you need, what support and upgrades are included. Also ensure the developer does regular updates.

Theme

Hire a web designer to create a custom theme to match your brand or download a free theme or purchase a premium theme and personalize it to match your brand.

The theme should allow you to add your logo, banner, and favicon and customize the sidebar(s). You can add widgets to change the layout of your website, add content, and create an awesome sidebar. You can also add a menu/navigation that makes sense. A good theme makes it easy to create a home page that passes the 3-second rule one that immediately captures interest.

Plugins

WordPress makes it easy to add and configure plugins.

Before creating your website you ensure you know exactly what you need it to do and research the plugins that will allow for that functionality. Some must have plugins include:
- Contact form
- Search Engine Optimization if not included in the theme
- Social Media - profile links and share buttons
- Google Analytics

Search Engine Optimization
Always configure your website for SEO, this may include adding a plugin.

Learn to Manage WordPress
Learn to add and edit pages, add images and blog posts. Manage and respond to comments on your website. Also, learn how to backup your website (this can be automated with a plugin).

WordPress is one of the simplest CMS to use and that's why I recommend it to clients and build the majority of websites on it. It empowers clients to be able to manage their own website.

Action Plan

Creating a rock solid alibi means setting up the backend properly.

NEW WEBSITE - If you are setting up a new website

- Choose and register a domain
- Find a hosting company
- Install or set up WordPress

- Read the next section to learn how to design and brand your website

EXISTING WEBSITE - Already have a website?

- Does your domain name represent your business as it is today? If not, consider a new domain name.
- Review your domain registrar. How are the service and cost?
- Review your hosting company? How are the service and cost?
- Use the next section to review and test the functionality and user experience of your website. Be prepared to make changes to your website if it no longer does what it needs to do to remain a money making website.

Action Plan

Chapter Four
The Crime Scene

Design and Branding

What clues did you leave at the crime scene? Don't butcher your design and slaughter your brand leaving a mess. Brand and design your website for optimal performance and sales.

Website Design

Website Rescue

The design section of this chapter is based on my free website assessment "Website Rescue" where I review your website based on user experience.

This is self-defence 101 for your website.

1. Take a look at your website from a visitors first impression view.

2. Non intrusive look to ensure your backend is configured properly to maintain your website to ensure no crashes, white pages or error messages.

I review design aspects that impact first impression, usability, and aesthetics. Design includes navigation, page titles, privacy policy, a consistent look and feel (branding) and color contrast.

The next section is validation. The quickest way to kill your website is with bad code or outdated programming. You also need to ensure that your website is mobile friendly in this day and age.

- HTML Validation
- CSS
- Javascript
- Speed
- Browser Compatibility

The third section is usability/user experience.
- Links
- Dead Links
- Font Size
- Contact Information
- Images

Make it easy to use and find stuff on your website.

The last section has three parts: content, social media and search engine optimization (SEO). I assess if your content conveys your marketing message and compels visitors to sign up or buy. Do you make it accessible by being easy to read? Is your content SEO friendly and shareable for social media? As you read through the design section have your website open and pretend like your viewing it for the first time.

We want to ensure your social media website integration compliments your web design. Before adding social media profile links and share button take into account branding (matches your brand) and layout (share buttons above the fold on shareable content). Do you have social media profile links on your website? Are your social share buttons functional and easy to locate?

Design

On a scale of 1-5 rate the following on your website.
1. Navigation is clear
2. Can tell automatically what website is about
3. Consistent look and feel
4. Necessary pages included
5. SEO friendly

Design for Clarity

Design isn't just about having a pretty website. You need to create a website that functions and serves its purpose. The following section shows how every aspect of your website can affect your sales and how you should always design with the end in mind. Remember, your website is a tool that attracts, converts and sells.

Poor design will hinder a website from making sales. People don't think that navigation, page titles, and content have anything to do with design. However, the layout and format of a website are equally as important as aesthetics. Too many web designers sacrifice usability for creativity.

- Navigation
- Page Titles
- Privacy Policy
- Consistent Look And Feel (Branding)
- Color Contrast

Navigation

The biggest source of frustration for web surfers appears to be the ability to find relevant information on a website - that's the biggest killer, the biggest driver of dissatisfaction. As soon as a web visitor is dissatisfied they will leave that website and defect to the competition. Navigation helps people find what they want.

Include a search field. Note that a visitor may skip navigation entirely and go straight to searching. Position your search field near the top of the page - either on the navigation bar or somewhere nearby.

Navigation should be identifiable and consistent. Make your navigation obvious and consistent. Don't change the main navigation depending on the page. This is not good, the whole purpose of the navigation element is to save readers from getting lost when they move about.

Links should be named in a way people expect. I am sure you have seen sites where the navigation links have been given "cute" names. Resist the self-destructive urge to "brand" your navigation. Readers won't click links they don't understand.

Link structure should reflect site structure. There are many sites with two navigation bars, and no clear difference between one and the other and people don't know what the difference is between them, or which one you think the page he's looking for should fall onto. Don't put the Contact page under an About section; readers don't expect that organization.

When most people think of web designers they think of branding and layout only. What they fail to realize, a good web designer thinks of how the navigation appeals to the visitor, makes sense and directs the visitors where they need to go.

Is your navigation clear, direct and free of confusing words?

Your site structure must be logical, and clear from a quick glance at your navigation. A reader must be able to see where on your site they are, and where they can go. If you have a lot of content to present, use a large drop-down menu that clearly breaks up your content into logical divisions (called a mega-menu), and breadcrumb navigation which shows readers where on the site they are: e.g., Products → Books → Website DOA.

Your site structure influences the navigation of the website and it's important to get it right the first time.

Site Structure - Don't overwhelm with your website menu. Most people's minds can hold 5 +/- 2 (i.e. 3-7) items of info at any one time. That's important when it comes to your website structure because it suggests that if someone has more than 5 +/- 2 options to choose between, they'll probably forget what the first option was before they get to the last one. Keep your menu and website options concise and simple.

Page Titles
Page titles are very important for your website for two reasons.
1. It tells search engines what the page is about - SEO

2. It tells visitors what the page is about.

Privacy Policy
Not only is a web designer concerned about content but I also want to ensure that you have all the necessary pages and that includes a privacy policy. Depending on your website's

objective, I have to determine what pages are required and how visitors can access these pages.

Branding

"Unattractive web design. Harsh colors, clashing colors, unreadable fonts, clutter - all these and more do not make an awesome website."

More about branding in the next section but you want your website to have a **Consistent Look and Feel** as well as **Color Contrast**.

When designing a website you also have to consider:
- Backend such as validation and SEO (is your website set up properly for optimization and for search engines to find you?)
- User experience - Are you using branding, aesthetics, and navigation to make your website easy to use?
- Content - How is the content laid out to make the most of it? How do you keep visitors on the page?
- Marketing such as social media - Are you making your website shareable and encouraging engagement?

Do's & Don't of Website Design

1. Don't use colors that clash - or blend in (use contrast)

2. Don't use flash or other animation

3. Don't use illegible typography - Use easy to read fonts, fonts sizes and font colors
4. Do have content above the fold

5. Don't automatically load audio or video - let visitors control start and stop

6. Don't open internal links in new browser window

7. Don't use graphics for text. Graphics increases the size of the web page and it's not Search Engine Friendly

8. Don't have too much material on page

9. Do use color on links - visitors should recognize what is clickable to easily navigate

10. Do you use a standard consistent layout

11. Do design for screen resolution currently 1020 x 788 - visitors don't want to scroll horizontally

12. Don't use too many images

Search #WebDOA on Twitter for a more comprehensive list and start following @DeathOfAWebsite

Validation

Users don't really care about validation but if your website is not properly configured it will break or be extremely slow causing you to lose visitors.

- HTML Validation
- CSS
- JavaScript
- Speed

- Browser Compatibility

HTML Validation, CSS, JavaScript

It is important that proper coding is used HTML, CSS, and JavaScript etc. This is the code that brings your website together. One bad line of code can break your website. You also want to ensure database connections are secure and up and running constantly. Using bad code on the server can cause your website to have multiple issues and error messages.

Validation is the responsibility of your web designer and if not done right, it will break your site. You can avoid validation issues by using a CMS such as WordPress and updating regularly.

Speed - see section on optimization for more information

On a regular basis you should ensure that you check your website speed and browser compatibility. If your site is too slow you will lose visitors and forget about return visits. If your site does not show up on certain browsers or devices then you will be losing again.

Browser Compatibility

As a web designer, I need to ensure a website looks just as good in Safari as it does on Internet Explorer as it does on a tablet or a smartphone. A mobile-friendly site is a must.

20% of consumers visit sites via mobile
11% make purchases using mobile
25% of all searches come from mobile devices
On a regular basis review your website on different devices and browsers. Make a note of the issues and if any error

messages pop up to bring it to the attention of your web designer.

User Experience

User experience is a big part of web design and should be a priority. Make it easy for visitors to come back again and again.

- Links
- Dead Links
- Font Size
- Images
- Contact Information

How many of you visit a website and can't find what you are looking for?

A good website focuses on user experience, fast to load, easy to read and easy to find what they are looking for. At the end of the day your website is not all about what you like and your wants and needs - your visitors have to be able to use the website and find it easy to use. A good website will have the proper coding so the site won't break, be fast, and allows you to view from multiple browsers and devices.

Many people spend a lot of money to design the website of their dreams forgetting that a website is not for them but the visitors, and potential leads and buyers that come to the website. In all the glitter and lights a website that is not user-friendly, or not accessible quickly turns people away.

Links

Do links open in a new window?

Dead Links

Is your website free from broken links or images? If you click on this underlined word, it should take you where you want to go. Links should be distinguishable between regular text. You want links that take you somewhere – No Dead links.

Font Size

You want the visitor to be able to read your website – Ensure font size applies to your target audience. The older the audience the larger the font.

Images

Understand that large images will slow your site. Text on images is not readable by search engines and in all marketing images must convey a message. Just don't stick an image in for no reason.

Contact Information

Don't make me have to search how to contact you. Must have a contact page – better yet add contact information to each page.

Making your website user-friendly a priority attracts more people and keeps people on your website longer.

Content

Besides having great content, you want to ensure your design compliments your content.

- Blog
- Easy to Scan
- Testimonials

Content

- Benefits
- Call to Action

The sad truth is there are still businesses that do not blog. Don't miss out on the opportunity to take your business to the next level with an updated regularly blog. Having an integrated, branded blog that's updated frequently draws in more visitors and is attractive to search engines.

Each page should be easy to scan. Remember 3 seconds. Make your content easy to read - format content for readability - short paragraphs, indentation, bullet points and the first sentence bolded in each paragraph.

By visiting your home page I should know immediately what you're selling. Every page should let me know why I should hire or buy from you. Effectively use benefits and testimonials to your advantage.

Ensure that every page on your site has a single, clear, unique purpose: Every page should have a call to action. So you have a website objective now take it a step further and have a page objective. What do you want visitors to do? Call, Email, Fill in the form, Download or Purchase? Tell visitors what you want them to do. Even after a blog post, it could be as simple as commenting or sharing via social media.

Make content marketing is a priority in your design to support and promote content.

Chapter Four

Social Media

Take advantage of the benefits of social media by integrating social media into your website.

Include your social media profile buttons on your website and integrate into your design by matching the visual branding. Many gurus will say don't put social media links on your website or at the very least remove from your home page because you are directing traffic away from your website. The fact is you get more engagement via social media than you do on your website. This is a great way to stay connected.

The easy and quickest way to engage visitors is to utilize social media sharing buttons on your website.

Also, don't forget to link your social media back to your website. I see that a lot. You go to someone's Facebook page and you don't see a website. You go to their website and you don't know they are on Facebook.

Increase engagement with your clients and visitors by integrating social media.

Search Engine Optimization

Search Engine Optimization is a large part of attracting visitors and having a successful website. Organizing your website by keywords is important. In the next chapter, we will dig deeper into keywords and onsite and offsite SEO.

Ensure that at the design state you make your website SEO friendly:

- Onsite Optimization
- Sitemap
- Robots.txt
- External Links
- Backlinks

Not only is your website structured for SEO but also for getting leads and making sales.
Be sure to optimize opt-in and sales pages.

When designing and creating content consider the objective of the website and keywords to use.

In the next chapter I dig deeper on how to SEO your website and how to properly use linking, sitemaps and robot.txt to make your website search engine friendly.

Branding
Website Brand

On a scale of 1-5 rate the following on your website.
1. Your domain relates to your business
2. You have your logo displayed
3. You have incorporated your colors in the website
4. The design appeals to your market
5. You have a favicon - adopt your logo or the initial name of your site

Does your website reflect your why?

Does your website reflect your current brand?

Chapter Four

Your website design should be in line with your business branding in every way.

Use your website to elevate your brand and increase brand awareness.

Before you even start building a website you have to ensure you have chosen the right domain name. Always choose a domain name that promotes your brand. If you are unsure about your domain, go back to choosing your domain section.

The next step is designing your branded website. Include your logo, favicon, and slogan/tag line and incorporate your brand colors.

Choose a design/ theme that reflects your business and appeals to your preferred client. The color, content, layout, graphics should reflect your business image.

Give your website a personality. Your website is a great place to reflect your voice. Inject your personality; showcase your perspective, philosophy and expertise.

Use your voice to stand out and start conversations. What tone, mood do you want your website to convey? How do you want them to feel? Ensure that your design and content reflects a consistent tone and mood in your own voice unique to you.

Don't hesitate to showcase your history, story, good news, celebrity endorsement, values, and information about you. Integrate this information into your design and let your personality shine in your brand.

Preferred Client

On a scale of 1-5 rate the following on your website.

1. Do you know who your preferred client is?
2. Does your website reflect your preferred client?
3. Does your copy speak to your preferred client?
4. Does your blog show results that your preferred clients are looking for.
5. Do you make it easy for your preferred client to share your website with others - building your Awesome Nation?

Your Preferred Client is NOT the only person you will work with.

Your preferred client IS the only kind of person you will spend your marketing time, marketing energy, or marketing dollars attracting to your business.

If you market for every one, you market to no one.

Who is Your Preferred Client?
- The people you most want to work with.
- The people who want, need and are willing to pay for what your business provides.
- Who would be the easiest clients to get?
- What group of people are you most comfortable with?
- Can you find them?

Research
The Internet makes it supremely easy to find data on just about any niche or segment of the population you can think of. In addition to the web you can use:
- Surveys/Questionnaires/Polls
- Interviews

- Observation
- Focus Groups
- Industry/Association Reports
- Your Competitors
- Current Client Perception

You can't please everyone. Your goals, marketing, and energy all align to reach your preferred client. Understanding your preferred client brings clarity to your business and makes it easy to write content and marketing materials.

<u>Download and complete the Market Research Worksheet in the Death of A Website Death of A Website Workbook and Planner and Planner.</u>

Know Your Client
Your audience is the targeted client base that you are hoping to reach out to for purchasing your products and services.

Demographics and Psychographics
- Gender
- Age
- Ethnic Group
- Relationship status
- Family
- Education level
- Work/Career
- Professional Experience
- Income/Discretionary Income/Earning Potential
- Talents
- Goals and Dreams
- Favorite Music, TV Shows, etc.
- Geographical Area
- Values important to them

Preferred Client

- Characteristics
- Priorities
- Hobbies and interest
- Work ethic
- Personality traits

A big part of knowing where they hang out is finding out who the influencers are.
- Who do they get information about their industry/niche from?
- What are they reading?
- What events do they attend?
- What groups are they a part of?
- What associations and organizations do they belong to?

By becoming a voice in the communities of influencers, groups and associations/organizations, you make it easy for yourself to be found and heard.

What Keeps Them Up At Night?
- How do they define success and failure?
- What's keeping them from their goals?
- What are perceived obstacles to their success?
- What are actual obstacles to their success?

Knowing and understanding your client allows you to provide better solutions as well as crafting your marketing to the issues.

How Does Your Product / Service Solve The Problem?
What outcomes/return on investment do they expect from your services or products?

You need to learn what words or phrases the clients use to describe the problem and find solutions to the problem. Using these keywords in your social media marketing will help you be found.

Why might they not buy from you? Identify the most common objections/concerns your preferred client might have about investing in your services or products.

Learn about your preferred clients buying process. Do they research potential purchases online? (If so, where?) Do they make the buy decision alone? Who else might they need input or permission from to make a decision? Knowing where your client is in the buying process and how they decide to purchase is a plus when drafting your blog and website sales copy.

Your Preferred Client Avatar

Once you have a solid understanding of who your target audience is and understand what their needs, interests, and goals are, use the information above to create your Preferred Client Avatar. Give your Avatar a name and create all your website content directed to your Preferred Client Avatar.

Meet Linda, my Preferred Client Avatar. Linda is a 38-year-old petite blonde. She is married and a mother of two beautiful girls. Linda is a reiki master, nutritionist, and speaker on wellness. She is the buyer and manages the finances in the family. Linda wants to do less one-on-one consulting and move to online courses. To do this Linda wants a new website and a social media strategy. She is worried that by making this transition, her family will have less money. Linda is a perfect candidate for my Awesome

Nation Allure program and the Awesome Nation Engagement Program. Linda can also become a consulting client. If Linda does not want to do it on her own she can choose my DFY – Done for You Services where we create her website and manage her social media.

Your Story

On a scale of 1-5 rate the following on your website.
1. Do you have an about me page?
2. Does your about me page relate to your clients and the products and services you are selling?
3. Does your about me page tell your story?
4. Is your about me page authentic?
5. Do you provide a professional photo so prospects can connect with you?

Your Story
A big part of successful Empowerpreneur branding is knowing who you are and letting others find out.

Know Your Why
What is the deeper meaning behind what you do?
I want to help _____ (your preferred client) get _____ (specific result) because it will help their life in what way _____ and this is important to me because _____ (how you want the world to change).

Use your website to get others behind your why.

Your Bio
Why do you do what you do?

How is your journey similar to your preferred client?
What adversity have you overcome that your preferred client
can relate to?
Remember to establish credibility - What are some top results
your clients have achieved?

Your Business
Give an overview of your business, how you got started, and
what makes you thrive today. The overview should be positive
and encouraging. It should also make potential clients think
you are an excellent person to buy from.

People buy from people. Use your website to get people to
know, like and trust you so they will eventually buy from you.
Create an about me page that tells your story in an engaging
way. Show people who you are with photos as well.

Your Offer

On a scale of 1-5 rate the following on your website.
1. Do you provide different levels of products and services
(Awesome Offer Mix)?
2. Do you provide content upgrades (Free Content)?
3. Do you make it easy to buy from you (2 clicks minimum)?
4. Do you have sales pages for offers?
5. Do you incorporate your offers in your blog?

What are you selling?

People will always invest in the following 4 things (the Big 4):
1. Money – how to make more, save more, spend less, attract
more

2. Relationships and love – save your marriage, find your soul mate, have better sex

3. Health and Fitness – lose weight, eat healthier, look younger, be sexier

4. Religion and Spirituality (this is a newer area) – being connected to something greater, a sense of community

WHAT you do for them (your gifts)

The products/services you offer is a combination of your gifts and your preferred client.

It's important to know who your preferred client is to get a clear picture of the "problem" that your gifts can "solve".

Use your website to let your prospects know the results or benefits a person can gain through your services. What are the benefits of the products and services you offer, and working with you personally? Why should someone choose you?

In getting leads and making the sales not only do you need to have the right offers, but your message to prospects and clients also have to be on point.

Your Awesome Offer Mix

In your Awesome Business you should have multiple offers which also provides multiple streams of income.

1. Your Lead Generating Offer (Awesome Free Gift) - quality eBook, checklist, event (teleseminar or webinar) video or audio

2. Your Discovery Session

3. Your Programs (results oriented systems) and Products (Do It Yourself Systems)
- Low-Priced products E-books or other
- Marketing and product sequence (upsells, cross-sells, and back end)
- Higher priced products, services and programs
- Create continuity programs such as memberships

Brand your products and services to be in line with your website branding. Use your website to promote your offers with multiple opt-ins and products sales pages. Create content on your blog that promotes your offers. Use your website to make it easy to buy. Turn your website into a sales machine by using the tools in the selling chapter.

Website Elements

How will your design bring cohesiveness to your website using color, fonts, patterns, and images? **Use the <u>website style sheet included in the Death of A Website Workbook and Planner</u> to outline colors and fonts.**

1. Have a recognizable **Logo**.
Create a logo that conveys who you are and what you do. Develop a logo use policy; have specific guidelines for how and where logo and tagline are used and how variations are used.

2. **Title** - Why should I read? What is the promise? Use H1 tags and color to stand out.

3. **Content** - Use formatted headings (H1, H2, H3), graphics/images, bulleted lists, columns, recurring and distinct brand elements in your content

Have blogging guidelines. **<u>Utilize blog post templates for the category, series and different blog post types included in the Death of A Website Workbook and Planner.</u>**

Create a blog style guide:
- Define what spellings and capitalization you will use.
- Inclusion and style of media (images, video, audio) in posts.
- Inclusion and access to downloadable resources.
- Text formatting including headings and subheadings.
- How you handle quotes, comments, and links.
- What SEO and Social Media elements to include.
- Outline the number of links per post, tweetable quotes and use of social media embeds.

4. **Images** - Have main and secondary post images for each blog category. Images of you are great for static pages. Create blog image templates utilizing text overlays, logo, and watermarks, etc. Also create social media images for blog posts.

5. **Elements** - Pattern styles, dividers, etc., Social buttons, icons, and images. Do the sidebar and footer have different graphics/images, rules, and guidelines?

When readers visit your blog they are drawn to two things:
1. How does it feel?

2. How easy is it to not only navigate but to use. Make it super easy to navigate, subscribe, comment, share and buy.

Bringing all these aspects together in a cohesive way relies heavily on the theme you choose. Choose an awesome theme for your website. You want a theme that is mobile compatible (responsive) and one that fits with your brand and has the tech capabilities that you want on your website. A client purchased a template that didn't allow for embedding plugins such as YouTube and wanted them to upload the videos instead which is not what they wanted. Long story short is do your research whether you are picking a template or getting a custom website you need to know what you want the website to do.

Check out other websites and themes. See what others are doing in your niche, what do you like and what don't you like? Also look outside the box and see what other niches are doing to get inspiration.

Action Plan

If you scored low on any of the design and branding questions it's time to rectify your website design and your brand.

Get someone not connected to the website to review.

Ask them the following questions:
1. Can you tell what the website is about right away?

2. Is the website easy to use?

3. Is the navigation clear?

4. Does the website seem slow?

5. Did you get any error messages?

6. Are you able to access on your mobile device?

7. Does the website look good on the mobile device?

8. Is the content easy to read and scannable?

9. Do you know what the benefits are for hiring me?

10. Do you know what I want you to do on each page?

Redesign and Rebrand Your Website If Required.

If your website scored lower than 4 on any section in the design start correcting it now.

Validation and Browser Compatibility

If your website is slow loading or has any error messages, you may want to get a web designer to review the website for validation errors.
If your website is not mobile compatible get a new theme now.

User Experience

If your website is not user-friendly make changes now to website structure and navigation.

Content

Content not matching your website or current brand? Start updating each page to match your brand. Consider updating each page to match your brand. Consider a redesign of your website. Add branded shareable images to the website.

Social Media
Is your website social media friendly? If not immediately add share buttons, and review and update content to make it shareable.

Search Engine Optimization
If your website is not SEO friendly add a SEO plugin or consider a redesign of a new website. Review each page and ensure you use Meta titles and descriptions that are keyword rich.

Does your website reflect your current brand?

Ensure your website:
1. Is visually branded (Colors, logo, favicon)

2. Speaks to your preferred client

3. Tells your story

4. Let's people know right away what you offer

Preferred Client - Create your preferred client avatar.

Your Story - Write down your story and a brief bio.

Your Offer - Brand your offer to match your website

Action Plan

Web Design Elements - Create your website style guide. **(Worksheet included in the Death of A Website Death of A Website Workbook and Planner and Planner)**

Contact Awesome Biz Online to get help with your branding. Take the Awesome Nation Allure Course.

Chapter Five
The Victim

Content

The first victim is usually the content. If for some reason visitors have found your website, ignored the issues with design and branding you have usually killed them with bad content, or no content. The quickest way to add value to your website is with content.

Must Haves

Website Must Haves

On a scale of 1-5 rate the following on your website.
1. Your homepage passes the 3-second rule
2. You have an updated about page
3. You have a contact page
4. You have dedicated (landing) service/product page
5. You have an updated blog

In addition to writing awesome content, there are some pages that every website must have. These must have pages serve as explainer pages and delve into details about who you are and your why. These pages help you build credibility, provide better user experience and increase conversion.

To attract visitors there are certain pages that you need to convey your information quickly in a concise way and visitors have come to expect these pages:
- Home
- About
- Work with Me (Brief Description of services with link to individual service page)

Services and Products (For Search Engine Optimization (SEO) purposes I recommend each offering has its own page)
- Testimonials
- Contact
- Blog

You must also include the following pages especially if you are capturing leads (peoples contact information) Terms of Use Policy, Disclaimer Statements, and Privacy Policy.

A branded website **Home Page** that immediately answers "what's in it for me".

About Page - After the home page, the second most visited page is your About Me page. People buy from people. The About page is a great page to start building trust. People want to know more about you and your business. This page also helps with branding and makes your website more personal.

Craft an awesome bio that allows people to get to know you and understand your why. Share your enthusiasm for your passion through the About page.

Resource Page - Include a resource page that includes a list of free and paid resources to help visitors to your website. Make this page have everything for beginners to expert level visitors.

Work With Me - If you are providing services, in addition to sales pages (more later), you need to include a Work With Me page. This page serves as a summary of your services and a big call to action to work with you.

Describe the services/packages you offer with an emphasis on benefits and results, have a clear call to action and add testimonials. Keep in mind your preferred client avatar when building this page and make it personable.

Testimonial Page - A big credibility booster to selling your own products and services is a dedicated testimonial page. Testimonials should be from actual people that are willing to endorse you. Testimonials should be results-focused and include full names and headshots.

Contact Page - Nothing is worse than going to a website and having to search for contact information. Again people buy from people. It's hard to make a buying decision if you aren't able to contact the seller. At the very least include a contact form that visitors can use to reach you.

Blog - Blogging is an awesome way to increase traffic, build your brand, attract leads, increase profits and make Search Engines happy.

The main reason you should be blogging is that it does increase sales.

The facts don't lie:
- 57% of companies with a blog have acquired a customer from their blog
- B2C's (Business to Consumers) with blogs generate 88% more leads per month and B2B's (Business to Business) generate 67% more leads per month
- 79% of online shoppers spend 50% of their shopping time researching products online.
Source: http://www.impactbnd.com

Optional Pages
- Events - Event Calendar
- Store - Shopping Cart (see e-commerce section)
- Speaking - Speakers Page
- Media - where your work has been featured where you have been featured in the media.

Having an awesome website will also attract opportunities such as JV / partnership invitations and media requests. Be prepared with the right content.

Home Page

The home page must be able to convey who you are, your why and what you are selling in 3 seconds since the attention span on the web is 3 seconds.

Use your home page to convey quickly:
- Who is your preferred client?
- What they are struggling with
- What they want instead
- What's possible?
- How you help them

Ensure your home page has a call to action. The number of websites that are beautifully designed with no clear call to action is a crime. Be clear about the objective of your website and tell visitors what you want them to do.

Optimize Your Home Page by using blog excerpts instead of full blog posts, use pagination and minimize the use of large images and video. Ensure your home page is not only attractive to keep people on your website but easy to navigate.

The less content you have on the home page – the faster it loads.

Website Pages

When developing content for your website think of structures and the routes that the readers can take from the page.

- Main Menu (Pages linked to from the main menu and navigation)
- Secondary (Second level pages supporting SEO and must have pages not included in the navigation)
- Additional (Supports the main menu and secondary pages and adds value)
- Extra (Internal pages that are not listed on the main menu and required pages such as legally required pages like the privacy policy).

Before developing the page know what is the purpose of the web page on your website? What is the benefit to the visitor?

Best Website Page Planning
Keyword Rich - One keyword you want to the page to rank for
Call to Action - One main call to action - What do you want readers to do after reading the page? Where do readers go next? Where do you want readers to go next? Do you want the web page to lead to an opt-in or a sales page?
What additional value can the page bring? Can you add a content upgrade?
What images support the content?
Is there supporting sidebar content?
What links does the page have internal and/or external?

Going in with a purpose and proper planning you can make every web page count.

Legal

Make your website is legal by adhering to Internet laws and local laws. Some pages that are legal requirements: Disclosure Policy, Privacy Policy, and Copyright.

If you make money from your site, you need to have a disclosure policy. Not only is it the law, but it's also the right thing to do! A disclosure policy lets readers know you are upfront about how you are making money.

Include links to your disclosure policy page at the bottom of your sidebar and in any sponsored post or post that contains affiliate links so that people can clearly see what your policies are.

If you collect any information from readers, you must also have a privacy policy. Most advertisers require a privacy policy and may drop you if they find you don't have one. It also lets visitors know how you plan to use their information.

Don't forget the Copyright; place your copyright at the bottom of your blog. In addition, include a copyright statement that clearly lays out what's okay and what isn't when it comes to others sharing pictures and copy from your blog.

Also include a Terms of Use Policy and Disclaimer Statements if required.

Have a lawyer review and approve all these policies and advise you of any other policies required.

Add this to your list of Must Have Pages to include on your website.

Plan Your Sidebar

Don't forget the sidebar is a great piece of real estate on your website. Review your website objectives. Do you want a sidebar that remains the same or changes depending on the section of the website or actual web page?

When planning your sidebar content, speak directly to your avatar and add value. Sidebar content should stand out, enhance your content and be clean and cohesive.

Go To Sidebar Options
- Opt-in box
- Awesome product image links
- Mini sidebar bio
- Include understated social media profile links if not a part of the footer

Use your sidebar and footer to draw attention to your opt-ins and products. Also, spotlight your most popular posts. People forget that these areas can also be used for navigation.

About Page

One of the most important pages on your website and the second most visited page is the "About Page".

The "About Page" can make or break a sale.

Your "About Page" isn't about you so much as it is about your preferred client and their challenges and desires, and the solution you offer that can help them achieve their goals.

Use your about page to Distinguish Yourself. You need to convey who you are, what you do and who you do it for. Get readers behind your why.

Here is a chance to show your personality and differentiate yourself. Use this page to make a connection and entice them to work with you and not your competition.

Grab attention with a compelling headline. Include a clear call to action throughout the page to lead them to what you want them to do next - check out your services, opt-in or buy. Include testimonials, celebrity endorsements, and mentions - any credibility builders.

Don't Fall into the It's All About Me Trap. If your website especially your home page has lots of "I", "Us", "We", "Me" then you have been caught. Make use of "You" and tell your readers what they will get from working with you (result). Remember always answer "What's in it for me?"

People buy from people. Include your bio, credentials, and your back story (if it relates to your results) and how they can get results working with you.

Resource Page

Provide a free resources page. This is a great opportunity to promote not only your own products and services but also tools that your preferred clients can use too. A resource page is also a money maker for any affiliate products that you are promoting.

Every product should have one or more free opt-ins that promote the product, and the resource page is a great way to showcase these opt-ins.

Use your resource page to direct visitors / preferred clients to solutions for the biggest problems that they face.

A delightful bonus of this page is that you can ensure that you reach people at any level of the buying cycle. You can include blog posts for people who are ready to buy now and blog posts for the people that are just beginning their research. Link to you most popular pages as well as your products and services.

Make it a landing page - no menu or side bar. Allow the resources to be focal on the page and include an opt-in form.

The resource page is great for increasing traffic and improving SEO (place emphasis on keywords you want to rank for).

The resource page may also be your greatest conversion page from reader to subscriber.

Reap the benefits of a well-planned resource page.

Content Strategy

Content

On a scale of 1-5 rate the following on your website.
1. You frequently update content on the site

2. Headlines are catchy and explain what the page is about
3. You provide information to visitors
4. You use keyword rich content
5. Each page uses a call to action

Content marketing is a very important part of online marketing. Content marketing is not only about blogging it includes:
- Home page and all other website pages especially the About Me page
- Videos
- Newsletter / Ezine
- Media pitches and press releases
- Advertisements
- Product descriptions (tell the story behind your product)
- Teleseminars/Webinars
- Books (print books or eBooks)
- Podcast
- Infographics
- Whitepapers
- And more

The biggest question with content marketing is what to write. Use content marketing to answer every question you have ever been asked about your business, products and services and what you do (great for SEO). It is a great opportunity to squash objections and showcase your expertise. With your content, you need to get really clear on who you are, who your preferred client is and the results you provide.

When writing content, take out your handy avatar and speak directly to your preferred client. What's important is the outcome, solution, and results - think about the clients wants and needs. What does a prospect need to know to turn into a client? Make all content relevant and useful to your preferred client. Always add value and think "what's in it for me".

Inject your voice (personality) into what you write as well build an emotional connection by making it personal to your readers.

When someone reads your website what do you want them to do next? Always include a call to action. One of the biggest mistakes I see Empowerpreneurs make in online marketing is that they are busy showing and telling, they forget to get engagement or ask for the sale.

With all online marketing have a content marketing strategy.

What's your overall objective and objective of each piece of content? How often are you going to publish? When? Use an editorial calendar to help keep you on track. Who will write/manage content?

Content Checklist

1. Write for SEO
- Use a keyword rich header
- Use keywords and a minimum of 300 words per page. This will increase your rank.
- Link to related content internally and externally.

2. Know your objective. Each piece of content should have one specific message and a call to action.

3. Provide fresh, valuable informative content about you, your products and services or your business.

- Make sure your content is easy to read, clear and concise.

- Your page uses bullets or numbered lists and subheadings to categorize and segment content and to make information standout

- Use images that relate to the content to reinforce your message

- Effective use of white Space around images and text

- Check spelling and grammar

4. Know your audience. Write targeted content.

5. Write for engagement. Give readers a reason to share and make it easy to share (share buttons) or comment.

Va Va VooM™

Use your content to market your products and services. Be careful and don't fall into the promotion trap. Your website/blog is your personal network television channel, but if you played commercials all day, you would have a lot fewer viewers.

Most marketing gurus toot a ratio for content marketing. How many informational posts vs. promotional posts? I promote 4 aspects in my **Va Va VooM™** content marketing approach that adds visual to the list because a huge part of successful online campaigns is the eye-catching image or the must watch video. According to the stats, people are more likely to engage with images and stop to watch videos.

Value – 60% - Tips, tutorials, useful and helpful posts.

Visual – 20% - Make use of images and videos - create branded images and video. Create pinnable and shareable images for your blog.

Voice – 10% - Show your personality - personal posts about you, showing your life and a behind the scenes look.

Marketing – 10% - Promotional posts to sell and promote your products and services

Use content marketing to promote your website. Make your blog work for you.

Blogging

On a scale of 1-5 rate the following on your website.
1. Do you have a blog?
2. Are you a consistent blogger?
3. Do you know what is your best blog category?
4. Do you know what blog post is the most popular?
5. Do you consistently share blog posts on social media?

Start using your blog to increase sales. If you don't have a blog yet, get started today!

Top 5 Reasons for Empowerpreneur Blogging

1. Client Appreciation and Loyalty

The easiest way for businesses to create blog content is to answer client questions. Using your blog to create an awesome library for clients builds loyalty. A blog is a great way to establish trust and can become an educational resource that keeps clients coming back. To ensure repeat visitors that will be repeat clients, blog honestly and subscribe to transparency in your blogging.

2. Lead Generation

By creating an awesome resource center with your blog, you will attract qualified leads. Creating keyword rich content will allow prospects to find you and good content will keep them coming back. Provide an opt-in form to turn these prospects into leads and these leads into clients.

3. Increase Search Engine Rankings

Google loves new content, especially new content that is keyword rich. Use your blog to generate inbound links and traffic by optimizing every post with your keywords. Google also indexes blog posts faster.

4. Increase Engagement

Use your blog as a promotional tool and share on social media. Use social media to attract new visitors and increase engagement. When you create a new blog post be sure to share on all your social media profiles. Also share your blog in your email marketing.

Quick tips for an Easy to Read Blog

1. Readable

2. Conversational Tone, use your voice

3. Use subheadings and bullet points to break up text and make it scannable.

4. Always add value

5. Use your blog to address each level in the buying process. Have blogs posts for new visitors and for visitors that are ready to buy now and those visitors that are in between in the buying process.

Your blog is not only a promotional tool for your website it is also a very effective communication tool for your prospects and clients.

What's the catch? The only "trick" to blogging is to be consistent and blog on a regular basis. There are no hard and fast rules around blogging. Some experts say blog every day, blog every week, or blog whenever you have value. You will get ten different answers on what to blog about, how long your posts are, what proportion of your posts are promotional... Everyone has an opinion based on what has worked for them.

How often do you blog? Search Engine Optimization relies heavily on content, new content, updated content and the more content you have on your website the more attractive you are to Search Engines.

When blogging develop a plan - create a blog editorial calendar. Decide in advance how often you want to write (frequency), how much (length - for SEO purposes aim for a minimum of 300 words) and what you want to write about (topics).

No matter what you decide make sure blogging is a part of your online marketing.

If you want more information on blogging read <u>Fall in Love with Blogging: From Passion to Plan to Profit.</u>

SEO

1. I know what SEO stands for
2. I have optimized my site for SEO
3. I have submitted my website to directories and search engines
4. I submit guest blog posts
5. I have a blog

All online marketing is SEO (Search Engine Optimization)

Use Search Engine Optimization (SEO) in Your Website Content Strategy

A properly search engine optimized website can increase traffic, subscribers, leads, and sales.

Keywords

While providing valuable content don't forget the importance of a keyword-optimized page. To be found online you must use the terms people are searching for to optimize your website. Whatever you're selling someone is buying. And these buyers are going to search engines to find you. You want search engines to index your pages (added to their databases), you want your website to be found for your keywords, and just like everyone with a website you want to be on Google's first page of results when someone uses your keywords.

Do your keyword research. What terms are people using to find you, your business, your website and your products and services? Pay attention to your Google Analytics organic search terms and use Google Adwords Keyword Planner. Turn long tail keywords into interesting questions and post ideas that appeal to readers. Long tail keywords are easier to rank for even though it brings less traffic it has a higher conversion rate. People that use long tail keywords to search are usually ready to buy. Every page of your website should be keyword optimized.

Optimize Your Page

Title The most important piece of SEO real estate on any website page is the title, which tells both readers and search engines what to expect from the rest of the content. Focus on one keyword per a page and ensure you have an enticing keyword rich title. Write for readers, not search engines. Go for readability while using relevant keywords in your titles.

You also have the **Meta Title** which may or may not match your post title especially when you may want to use a different title for readers than for search engines. Your title for search engines may differ in the use of keyword at the front and a simplified version to fit within the 70 characters. However, it still has to be appealing as this is what people will see on search engines.

Meta Descriptions are also important as this is what search engine users will see when your result pops up and on social media as well. The description needs to inspire users to read the blog post as well as contain the keywords used to search for it.

To edit meta data, you need to have a theme framework or plugin installed that provides a place for specific SEO meta data.

Ensure your website utilizes meta data and incorporates open graph, schema.org and twitter cards. These tools allow social media and search engines to better classify and display information from your website.

Slug / URL Don't use automatically generated URLs. Ensure you URL is search engine friendly with keywords while being reader-friendly - easy to read, and understand. If you sent only the link to someone would they be compelled to click and read? Also, think compact - shorter URL's (less than 100 characters) are easier to copy, paste and share.

Links Linking is a great way to build relationships while increasing SEO rank. When you link to others not only do you get linked back you also get mentioned as well. Internal linking also helps with optimization and keeping happy readers on your website. The key to linking is optimized links with keywords - don't use "click here", say what the link is and ensure links are helpful - think resources.

Images Rename images to describe the actual image, instead of IMG23.jpg use sunset-toronto.jpg. Take it a step further and optimize for SEO with keywords - what is the blog post about? Ensure you are uploading the proper size, instead of relying on WordPress to scale the image upload the size you want. Large images slow down the site. Finally use search engine optimized title and alt tags that use the post keywords. Pinterest uses the alt tag as the image description. Videos and other rich media content types

The key to using images is ensuring that it's relevant and adds value to the post.

Valuable Content

Create valuable content. If your content sucks and no one wants to engage or read it, then SEO will not help you.

Share unique content. Readers are more likely to engage with fresh content.

SEO is a large part of how you will organize your website. Review navigation and page structure.

Be active. Post regularly. Use your blog to keep top of mind in your industry, in the eyes of potential clients as well as in search engines.

Offsite SEO

Cultivate your ranking with offsite SEO by submitting your website to Search Engines and blog and website directories. Also use linking to your advantage - Search Engines like it when you reference other websites (external links) and your own pages with internal links - just make sure it is related. You can consider Paid Search is an option as well, where you pay to have your website pages listed in Search Engines and directories. Pay Per Click (PPC) ensures you appear higher on search results and you only pay when someone clicks on your link as opposed to Cost Per Impression (Cost per Mille - CPM), when you pay for the amount of times your link/ad is shown.

SEO Maintenance

The last step is to maintain your SEO by using tools like Google Analytics. On a regular basis, you want to keep on top of your SEO by making adjustments and reviewing your metrics.

Search Engine Optimization – Please note with any SEO campaign you will see results in 4-6 months. Don't think you can optimize your site and voila it's on the first page of Google.

Search Engine Marketing Process

At Awesome Biz Online I use the proprietary CARE™ process that I developed.
C – Consult
A – Analysis and Research
R – Review and Report
E – Evaluation

Consult

We learn more about you, your products, services and business

Analysis And Research

- **Keyword Analysis** Keywords and key phrases to get search indexing
- **Keyword Research** find the keywords with the best results
- **Research** Industry and Competition, Traffic and Geographical target

- **Site Analysis** Meta, Content, Theme, Speed, Layout and Structure
- **Social Media Analysis** Visibility, branding, traffic, engagement, consistency and frequency

Review And Report
- **Standard Compliant Mark-up** No Syntax errors and does conform to strict XHTML markup based on W3C standards and CSS
- **Semantic HTML** Describe type of data on pages – semantically appropriate HTML elements and tags enable Search Engines to know the difference between heading and sub-headings
- **Link Optimization Strategies** Review inbound links, link popularity and ROI
- **Submission** - daily submission and sharing
- **Monthly Maintenance** Tweak, Defend your placement
- **Report** Monthly Progress Reports and Final Report

Evaluation
- Organic Optimization
- Size and complexity of site
- Page rank and backlinks to site
- Size of brand/organization
- Difficulty of project
- Competition ranking

Anyone can have their unique business name on top of the Search Engine, but the real value is having your site come on top when customers search for the keywords that describe your business, products or services.

No one can guarantee you #1 ranking. Any company that does, stay away. We can guarantee professional, ethical SEO strategies for your website.

The best SEO strategy for you depends on how much competition there is for your key phrases, your target audience, and global and local

We recommend to all our customers that they enrol in our SEO Maintenance program to ensure that listing stays on top

Marketing Message

On a scale of 1-5 rate the following on your website.

1. Marketing message is clear throughout site
2. Relay the benefits and downplay features
3. Call to action is clear
4. It is clear who your preferred client is
5. You have a USP

It's easy to get caught up in the buy now, hire me cycle but you have to ensure that you consistently provide value to your website.

Create a marketing message that resonates and is at the root of all your content.

Remember you why:

I want to help _____ (your preferred client) get _____ (specific result) because it will help their life in what way _____ (lifestyle results/benefits) and this is important to me because _____ (how you want the world to change).

You want a marketing message that attracts, qualifies (speaks to your preferred client) and directs people where you want them to go. It's important to know your business objective - clearly define your website objective.

Always keep your preferred client avatar front and centre when writing. Remember problem, symptom and result. What are their fears, goals, and desires? What does your audience want/need to hear?

WHO you work with (your preferred client)
- Think back to your preferred client avatar
- The urgent problems of your preferred client
- The symptoms (What behaviours do they exhibit?)
- The progression (What problems they currently have that lead to other problems?)

Getting the right message about your offers to capture leads and convert leads into sales is very important. A big part of conversion is having the right copywriting. The right copy can help you increase sales on your website

Be clear, concise with the benefits of you and your business. Benefits should be as explicit and specific as possible

- What problems do you solve?
- What symptoms of pain do you address?
- Make them quantifiable. Quantifying your benefit statement means translating it into numbers or actual quantities of things that your ideal client can relate to. It might be dollars, hours, days, tips, secrets, solutions, etc.

Putting value before sales wins every time. Value makes return readers, and gets readers to know, like and trust you so they will buy.

Writing Your Marketing Message

What's your USP?

What's in it for me?
- Target market
- Problem of target market (symptoms, issues, needs and wants)
- Solution (who are you and unique solution)
- Results (Price /proof - case studies and testimonials)
- Different from competition

Your USP can be your slogan/tagline.

Do all your web pages relay your USP?

Eliminate Competition

Niching down is a way to eliminate competition. Your niche makes you stand out in the crowd. It makes you memorable. You attract people that want the solutions you offer.

Take the time to research competition. Learn what makes them different, and why clients should choose you.

Many businesses fail because they do not consider their competition. You need to do proper research about your competitors, learn what makes you different, why the customers should choose you, and much more.

What Makes You Different?
- What differentiates you from your competition?
- What value do you bring to your prospects?
- How does choosing you benefit your clients?
- Why do they like you?
- Why do they buy from you?
- How can you capitalize on your differentials in your social media?
- How are you similar?
- Do they have the same products and services as you?
- What types of online advertising do they use, are they successful?
- What is their campaign fails?

The perfect marketing message relays who you are, tells people your why, who are you writing for, the problems you solve and why you are unique. Spend time crafting the right message.

Action Plan

Content
Do you have the Must Have Website Pages?
- Home
- About

- Work with Me (Brief Description of services with link to individual service page)
- Services and Products (For Search Engine Optimization (SEO) purposes I recommend each offering has its own page)
- Testimonials
- Contact Page
- Blog
- Legal Pages

Review each page to see if you meet the content criteria. Create a schedule to start updating content now.

Does your homepage convey who you are, your why and what you are selling in 3 seconds? If not start revising your homepage.

Review your website structure is it set up to take the reader where you want them to go?

Take stock of your current sidebar. Make a list of the items currently in your sidebar. Does it serve your website objectives and the needs of your visitors? Does it seem necessary? Does it stand out or get lost?

Review your about page. Is it about you or **your clients**? Update it now.

Create a resource page that focuses on the biggest problems and desires your preferred clients face.

Blogging

Do a regular blog audit and review your top 10 most popular posts. What keywords were they optimized for? Create new content keeping these keywords in mind.

Download and complete the Blogging section in the Death of A Website Workbook and Planner.

5 Day SEO

Day 1 – Keyword Research
- Use the Google Keyword Planner
- Review your analytics
- Optimize or update five pages on your website

Day 2 - Comment on 5 blogs

Day 3 – Participate in 5 forums (don't forget to add your signature)

Day 4 – Write a press release, post it on your site and submit to FREE PR banks

Day 5 – Guest Post on related blogs

Go through the 5-day cycle for a month spending up to half an hour a day and reap the rewards. You will see a better Google ranking for your efforts.

Marketing Message

Does your content convey your marketing message?
1. Write down your marketing message and keep it where you can see it when you write content for your website

2. Review each page to ensure that you are relaying your marketing message. Now look at the main pages of your site.

Do you see your marketing message? Is it clear to the visitor, who you are, and what you do, who you help and how you help them?
Write down the benefits of your company, product/services.

Read your web copy does it tell the visitor what the benefits are?
Think of ways to incorporate your benefits on the main pages of your website.

What are your features?
Have you incorporated the features on the site?
How have you downplayed the features? – Do you have a features page?

What is your call to action?
Now, look at the main pages of your website.
Is it clear what the visitor must do once they have visited your website?
Go back to the objective of your website. Are you accomplishing this with your call to action?

Are you relaying your USP?

List your top 3 competitors and do your research. How are you different?

Action Plan

Chapter Six
The Suspects

Selling

The first suspect is usually the "pushy salesperson" that only says buy now! Don't commit the buy now offence. Turn your website into a sales funnel without being offensive.

Lucrative Game Plan Questions

I developed the "Lucrative Gameplan" that takes a hard look at your website and results in a 50-page analysis and step by step guide that moves your website from an expense to a profitable tool. Website Rescue is from the user point of view and the Lucrative Game Plan is from the sales and marketing perspective.

When you implement the strategies from the Lucrative Game Plan analysis and report you will attract new clients, Increase sales and repeat business.

The Lucrative Game Plan is based on the Lucrative Marketing System which is based on my sales funnel.

Lucrative Marketing System:
- Traffic
- Capture Leads
- Nurture Leads
- Convert Leads
- Close, Deliver, and Satisfy
- Referrals

With the Lucrative Marketing Game Plan on top

- Google Ready
- Website Design

- Lead Capture
- Conversion

The first step is evaluating your website by completing the 20 point Lucrative Game Plan Checklist. It identifies where your website is now and how it can be improved. **Download and complete The Lucrative Game Plan Checklist.**

Review your score.
MINOR INJURY 19-20 make any necessary changes.
STABLE BUT CRITICAL - 15-18 Call me and I can help you score higher.
ON LIFE SUPPORT - Less than 15 call me immediately.
No matter the score take action and call.

I will provide a 50 page Lucrative Game Plan report showing you the exact step-by-step process to turn your website into a profit centre.

In the previous chapters, you reviewed many aspects of making a website profitable. The Lucrative Game Plan takes into account the following

1. Google Ready
Use SEO to rank on Google. Targeted keywords
I review your SEO and provide action steps.

2. Website Design
Your website may be the first impression you make. As we seen in the previous chapter Design not only includes visual branding, an appealing website but also the backend is properly configured to have a website that works.

Pass The Eye Test
Ensure that your website colors not only include your brand, you also have to ensure that the design/web page has flow and that each page has focus.

Effective Use of USP
Ensure that your website conveys your Unique Selling Proposition. What makes your business special?

Website Design Analysis - Much like this book I will provide action steps to improve.

3. Lead Capture & Follow Up

Lead capture and follow up processes are effective when using opt-ins, with an autoresponder.
This may be the most important section of the report because the money is in the list.
I review your lead capture process and provide action steps.

4. Conversion

Your website is a starting point for turning prospects into clients. You can also use it to create repeat clients. You can build trust and rapport by providing valuable information on your website and creating conversion tools such as free reports, content upgrades, videos, checklists, etc.
I review your sales conversions and conversion tools and provide action steps.

Finally, I provide you a list of top 3 priorities I recommend you do right away. The Lucrative Game Plan is devised so you can do changes in-house or bring it to your current web designer. After it's delivered, we offer 30 days of support to answer any questions you may have. If something is unclear, a question on how to implement a specific idea, I am here to help. Awesome Biz Online is available to implement the strategies listed and I am available after 30 days to consult with you on any of the strategies listed in the 50-page report.

Sales Funnel

Many people find it hard to create a sales funnel online because a lot of online advertising only target people that want to buy now and they are trying to duplicate what others are doing. Sadly that works for companies like McDonald's, but that's only 3% of the market. At any given time 47% will never buy, and 50% will buy in the next 12 months. It's not very effective to market to all 100% when you will only get a 3% return, and it's a broken marketing system. Basically, you are attracting traffic to your website and going straight into the sales pitch. Traffic - Website - Sales.

The goal of creating clients via your website is to capture leads so you can build a relationship that will lead to not one purchase, but to multiple purchases and referrals.

Take a step back use your website to create a sales funnel that works. Traffic - Capture Leads - Nurture Leads - Convert Leads - Close, Deliver, Satisfy - Referrals.

By being clear about your preferred client you automatically eliminate the 47% who will never buy. You want your sales copy and opt-in offer to get rid of these people; you want your autoresponder to weed out these people. Don't be sad when you lose subscribers - these are the people you don't want.

Blogging is a great way to capture the attention of people that are not ready to buy today but plan to buy. Use your blog to keep people coming back and keep you top of mind for when they are ready to buy. Attract leads by using opt-in offers and content upgrades in your blog posts.

Use **Va Va VooM** to promote your offers when blogging. Send promotional offers to your email list (and social media), make offers during live consultations, and make offers during webinars.

So now people are ready to buy from you either they are part of the 3% that come to your website or your blog reader or part of your mailing list.

Have a clear path to order. Ensure that prospective clients can find your order form/sales page quickly and easily. You never want to make them hunt for the buy button.

Clear Path To Order
- Create sales hubs
- Send promotional offers to email list (and social media)
- Make offer during live consultations
- Make offer during webinars
- Have exclusive product launches and events for your list
- Ensure that prospective clients can find your order form/sales page quickly and easily.

Don't forget to have landing and sales page metrics where you track links, and do split testing and track sales conversions.

The final step of your sales funnel is to have a referral and loyalty program. Create a referral program by sending samples copies to bloggers, influencers and friends. You can also create your own affiliate program.

There is no doubt that convincing your prospects purchase from your website is a hard job! But have you ever considered that you could be making the process more difficult? This is especially true if your site is poorly designed and you have weak content and sales copy.

Call to Action

On a scale of 1-5 rate the following on your website
1. Clearly tell users what you want them to do
2. Create a sense of urgency (deadline)
3. Above the fold (top of the page)
4. Call to Action on every page
5. Follow through - thank-you page or email

Include a sales nudge in your copy.

It's not a hard sell but direct your website audience to your products and services. A sales nudge are gentle reminders that you have products and services for sale as well as a way to build desire and curiosity.

For example "Be sure to download the (content upgrade) but if you want a more intensive something Sign up for the Awesome Nation Allure course. "

Create a sales nudge for each product. It can be subtle such as adding links to your products in your posts.

Call to Action

Using your website to post regular Awesome content is great, but it's not going to bring you the big bucks. Valuable content can drive visitors, and even engagement but alone won't drive sales. You need to encourage readers to take action.

1. Engage
2. Subscribe
3. Buy

Determine what you want readers to do after reading your blog posts.

What do you want people to do? Tell them!

What do you want your readers to do? Call, Email, Download or Purchase? Tell readers what you want them to do. With each post add a call to action. Click here, like, comment, share, etc.

Use **Va Va Voom** to create a mix of promotional posts, value add posts (printables and downloads) and information.

Each page should have its own call to action - define the main objective for each page. Does your call to action align with your website objective? Is it an introductory offer, free gift, guarantee, or content upgrade?

When crafting a call to action or a sales nudge consider "what's in it for me" what do you want readers to do right now? Use your call to action to compel your readers to take action. Use active language - Call, Buy, Request, Submit, Donate, Download. Must communicate what will happen, when you click.

An effective call to action should stand out. Add space around it, bigger font and use colors to draw attention. Review design such as size, color and position.

Communicate urgency in your call to action - Most people react out of fear of missing out (FOMO)
- Now
- Today
- Act now
- Limited time only
- Limited quantity
- Enter soon
- On sale
- This week only
- Don' miss out
- Etc.

Follow through, ensure there are immediate results based on the call to action. Include the "Thank you" page, autoresponder email, etc.

List Building

On a scale of 1-5 rate the following on your website.
1. You have an opt-in on every page
2. You have specific landing pages just for opt-ins
3. You have content upgrades to build your list
4. You have a call to action to subscribe to your mailing list
5. You track and analyze your opt-in offers

Are you actively building your email list and tracking opt-in rates?

The quickest way to increase sales is to create your list. And the quickest way to build your list is with an Awesome Gift. The Opt-in aka the Awesome Gift: Ebook, Checklist, Event (Teleseminar, Webinar or Live Event, Video or Audio Class) is a great way to capture leads and build your list.

The Free Offer - Opt-in - Awesome Gift is an INCENTIVE.
The offer must be valuable and relevant to your preferred client.
Don't offer crap, a real value of at least $100 goes a long way of turning subscribers into buyers.

A list builds relationships and nurtures loyalty.

Create a List Building Hub

Opt-in Boxes - Have an Opt-in form above the fold and/or in the top right corner, use an action popup (on entry and/or exit)

Opt-in Page - Use a focused landing page to convert readers. A landing page removes other distractions that hinder reader action (no menu, header, logo) and has only one call to action. This dedicated landing page can be used for traffic from advertising and social media. Use landing pages to emphasize what you are promoting; I recommend a landing page for each marketing campaign. Remember, your landing page has only one clear call to action.

Confirmation Page / Thank-you Page - Thank and welcome them, inform them that the registration is complete and deliver free content.

Autoresponder Emails - Nurture Leads and Build Relationships - Create a 7-12 message autoresponder for your List Building Hub. Ensure that emails are created to build trust and provide valuable information. Use your autoresponder sequence to educate.

Next, use this opportunity to promote your offers, launch products and services, offer other freebies, invite feedback, and drive traffic to your website. Remember Va Va Voom. Use your list to get prospects to like, know and trust you. This is the perfect way to turn leads into sales.

Drive Sales and Leads
- Opt-in box on EVERY POST
- Link to your products/services on EVERY POST
- Feature case studies/testimonials
- Make it easy to contact you and/or order
- Make it easy to share you
- Drive more traffic to the list building hub
- Create more free content and hubs as needed
- Track and test for your most successful offers and traffic sources

Services

Services On a scale of 1-5 rate the following on your website
1. My services have their own web page
2. Image
3. Call to action is clearly defined
4. Form to capture leads
5. Customer proof (testimonials, sales letters)

Building the perfect service/product/sales page comes with knowing and understanding sales copy.

From a design perspective you want to ensure that the page is just like a landing page (no navigation, or sidebar) - remove any clutter so readers can focus on your offer and take action.

Get clear on your preferred client. This page must speak directly to the problem that you can solve for your preferred client. When the preferred client visits the page, they know right away you are speaking to them, it should be clear who exactly the service is for.

Let your service/sales be very clear about the promise, outcome, result they will get from hiring you.

HOW you do it (your process/methodology)
What do you do with your clients? What are your guiding principles and your process (system)? How do you deliver your gifts and/or how does your preferred clients digest information (audio, pdf, video, etc. or a combination). How long does it take?

Take advantage of white space. Your sales/service page must have one specific objective, one goal, one action. Content revolves around the action and design and copy speaks to the audience and focuses on the call to action.

Always display the first call to action above the fold.

Every Offer Must Haves
- Headline - compelling keyword-rich clear headline
- Enticing Images

- Benefits - Results / What's in It For Me
- Bonuses
- Testimonials - You should have testimonials, written and video, on every page of the site especially your service page. (There are no guarantees that they will visit the testimonial page or this service page.).
- Call to Action
- Guarantees - The majority of customers will not request a refund, especially if you are offering a quality product. However, if they do request a refund make sure the process is quick and easy as well.
- Multiple Payment Options - Offer multiple payment options. Some people may feel comfortable paying via PayPal, some may only want to pay with their credit card and others might want to send a check. The more options you offer, the better your chances of covering your prospects' desired payment method.
- Easy Way to Purchase - use a reputable payment processor/shopping cart and prominently display the buy button.

Ensure Your Sales Page Answers The Most Important Questions
- What is this product/service?
- Why do I need it?
- When do I get results?
- How do I order the product/service?
- When does the product/service arrive?
- How much is it? Is there a payment plan available?
- What is included?
- Is there a guarantee or return policy?
- Why is this different from Joe Schmoe's product/service?
- What will they achieve?

- What is the product/service
- How long does it take? Is it time released (weekly, monthly)?
- How is content delivered? How do they access content?
- Is there a community/group coaching aspect via Facebook group or forum?
- Pricing and Payment - What is the cost? IS there payment plans? Is there a refund policy?
- What are your terms of enrolment (application)?
- Any discounts, early enrolment, specials?
- How is it delivered? PDF, video, etc.

For some reason people may be hesitant to buy from your awesome sales page. Don't let them leave empty-handed. Create an opt-in on the page, either have a box, a link to click to a landing page or a pop-up. Get them to register, tell a friend, subscribe or buy (upsell or cross-sell).

Download and complete the Services section in the Death of A Website Workbook and Planner.

Products

Products On a scale of 1-5 rate the following on your website
1. Products have detailed descriptions
2. Products list benefits
3. Products list features
4. Call to action is clearly defined
5. I have online promotions around my products such as incentives/bonuses

As a service based business make the leap to offer products and increase your potential for multiple streams of income.

You can easily add products to your website without a full e-commerce solution (covered in next section).

Consider adding:
- Planners (physical and PDF)
- Ebooks/Books
- Merchandise (branded T-shirts mugs etc.)
- Complementary products
- Training products
- In between - maintenance products

All your offers are based on the problems that your preferred clients have where you can provide the solution (results).

Your Offers Must
- Educate
- Build Trust
- Talk to the Pain
- Create Urgency
- Showcase Results
- Have a Call to Action

For Every Offer Create a Kickass Sales Page Hub
When visiting a lot of Empowerpreneur websites they forget to cater to the 3% that are ready to buy now, that's a quick way to lose prospects. Create a dedicated sales page where people can make a purchase now.

Don't turn away customers as they are ready to buy. Every product or service should have a Sales Hub that includes:

Products

Opt-in Boxes - For every offer create a pre-launch mailing list by offering a free webinar or download related to your product.

Sales Page - Create a branded sales page that has the product logo and colors. Include the branding on all your sales and marketing material for the offer.

Benefits are a huge differentiation factor. Emphasize the benefits in your sales copy - "What's in it for me?" The features of your products and services are also important and they go hand in hand with the benefits. The features of a specific product should provide a benefit. How can you turn your features into benefits?

Consider creating sales videos, bonuses, free training, webinars and giveaways, and an affiliate campaign to promote your product.

BONUS: Offer an unadvertised bonus.

Just like the service sales page, make it easy to buy and include the call to action above the fold.

Always up-sell similar or related products.

Just like your service sales page, you want to include offer must haves on the sales page and include the most important questions. For both product and service pages you also want to include an FAQ section.

Frequently Asked Questions on Your Sales Page

When a prospect is interested in what you offer as a product/service, she comes to the table with questions. Online you're not there to answer those questions so you have to anticipate what those questions might be to overcome potential objections in the copy. Those are the frequently asked questions or FAQs section.
- Who?
- What?
- Why?
- When?
- Where?
- How?
- How much?
- Offer?
- Guarantee?
- Objections?
- Terms of service
- Does it come in different colours?

Delivery Page / Thank-you Page - Thank and welcome them, inform them that the registration is complete and deliver the product or set in motion delivery with an auto delivery system.

Be sure in delivery you delight and satisfy the client. You can have the best product/service but if there is a problem getting the product and they have a shitty experience it does not matter.

Autoresponder Emails / Follow up - Always keep a separate list of buyers. Definitely, include a Sales Follow Up Auto-Responder. Send a thank you / confirmation email with details for accessing the product and getting support. Don't forget to send an email receipt, followed by instructions on how to use, followed by a 7-12 message autoresponder messages. The first 3-5 messages reinforce the sale, help clients use the product or access the service and remind them how to get support. Remember **VaVaVoom**.

Have ready a customer service process with a refund system.

For every new offer create a launch plan and a marketing plan. Reach as many prospects as possible - go for excitement and impact.

<u>Download and complete the Products section in the Death of A Website Workbook and Planner.</u>

E-Commerce

On a scale of 1-5 rate the following on your website
1. Secure shopping cart
2. Retrieve contact info
3. Do not store credit card and other related information online
4. Pages around delivery, returns and privacy
5. Featured Product/Related Product

Could you benefit from having an online store?

Not only can you reach a larger audience online and geographically you can give existing clients an opportunity to return and by from you again and again.

1. Store design and layout. Include a branded e-commerce store.

1. Logo and graphics to match rest of website

2. Branded products

3. Themes - consider WooCommerce theme or plugin for WordPress (I use WooCommerce plugin with StudioPress theme) you can also consider other platforms such as Shopify.

2. Store Management

Whatever shopping cart/e-commerce system you choose, ensure that it's user-friendly not only for potential clients but for you too. The number one reason why people abandon shopping carts is because it's too complicated to manage. Ensure it's easy to customize and brand. It also needs to have the functionality you need. Before I quote on an e-commerce website I need to know the specs and what capabilities the online store needs to have.

Security - Security is at the top of any e-commerce store. How you handle payment (credit card information), as well as private information from buyers needs to be up front and included in your policies. You should have a proper security setup that includes an SSL certificate.

Payment - Ensure you can secure payments and use a reputable company - what payment methods/gateway and/or merchant account will you employ?

Tax - do you collect taxes (how much)?

Inventory - how many products? Do you have a physical location and will you maintain separate inventory online. Will you use the built-in inventory management system?

Shipping - where will you ship to? How do you ship? Consider shipping options such as flat rate, free shipping, local delivery, and instant download. You can also integrate third-party shipping to calculate shipping automatically. This is a big fail for new online retailers as they incorrectly calculate shipping costs and forget to include shipping supplies.

Policy - It's very important to create policies for your e-commerce website. Include pages on your website for privacy, shipping, returns and exchanges, and customer service. In some countries it's illegal not to include these very important pages.

Customer Service - Not only do you want to have easy to find policies on your website you also want to provide top notch customer service. The goal is to have your website working while you sleep.
- Ensure your website is able to answer all the questions (Consider a store FAQ section in addition to product FAQ)
- Have template emails to answer questions
- 24 hour response time

Download E-Commerce Checklist for a Comprehensive List

3. Search Engine Optimize store and products.
Product name + keyword + company name
Meta description
Product description
- Short description can be used for meta and may be featured next to the product on category pages (excerpt)

- Product details are included in the long product description - aim for 300 words for SEO, and get ranked for long tail keywords. Also optimize product category.

4. Product Details

Product Name - compelling keyword-rich clear product name

Category - clear, concise, SEO category

Description - clear, concise, engaging and complete

Featured image - main product image (consider professional product photography)

SKU - product number or barcode number

Price - regular price and / or sales price listed

5. Easy Marketing Boost - promote other products while selling
Include product reviews section and encourage reviewers.
Cross-sell related and complementary products.
Upsell other products and accessories.
Include bonuses.

6. Don't Make These E-Commerce Mistakes
- Charge too much for shipping
- Slow website
- Complicated buying process
- Cross-sell or upsell irrelevant
- Horrible or no images
- Pricing hidden - need to be transparent

- Product availability - communicate early in the buying process, also an effective marketing tool to build urgency
- Website functionality - up to users expectations
- Lack of shipping information
- Bad navigation

These are the 6 areas to consider when you want to add e-commerce to your website.

For a Comprehensive List, Download E-Commerce Checklist.

Action Plan

1. Check your score on the Lucrative Game Plan Checklist

2. Review your online sales funnel

3. Are you implementing the online sales funnel?
Review and update areas where you are weak.
Put systems in place

4. Add call to action on every page where appropriate

5. Create your list building hub

6. Opt-in offers / test options

7. Autoresponder / test options

8. Create and promote service sales pages

9. Create and promote product sales pages

10. Consider an e-commerce system or if you already have e-commerce in place - download the checklist and review your system and processes.
E-commerce/shopping cart

11. Review your landing and sales pages

12. Review/create your customer service and policies. Are the current ones still relevant? What are the laws in your area?

Action Plan

Chapter Seven
The Evidence

Marketing

Every criminal leaves evidence. This time lead a trail to your alive and kicking website with effective marketing.

Get Found

On a scale of 1-5 rate the following on your website.

1. I post my website address on directories
2. I post my website address on business cards
3. I post my website address on all communications and marketing material
4. I include my website on all my social media profiles
5. I have submitted my website to search engines

8 Simple Ways to Get Found Online

1. Submit your website to search engines

2. Submit your website to niche and industry directories

3. Include website on social media profiles

4. Include your website on all marketing collateral
- Print Materials
- Business Card
- Flyers
- Postcards
- Trade Show Banners
- Thank you cards
- Appointment cards
- Brochures
- Presentation Folders
- Letterhead

- Envelopes
- Invoices
- QR codes

5. Have any news? Create a press release.

6. Take SEO seriously. Review your titles, meta description and ensure they are not only keyword rich but also enticing

7. Consider setting up an affiliate program and get others to advertise your website. Build a network of affiliate links to promote your site. Pays commission to other site owners for actual sales

8. Track Marketing with URLs
Create a unique URL for each separate piece of advertisement

9. Tell people. When talking to people promote your website and handout your marketing collateral to promote it.

Get Local

Another great way to promote your awesome website is to promote it to the people in your community. A website is a great way to go global but don't forget the people around you.

Identify and Partner with Neighbourhood Blogs
Guest blog post on neighbourhood blogs and those from surrounding areas. Showcase your business, blog about being a business owner in the neighbourhood and add your events.

Local News

Local newspaper, free paper, or news TV shows will always be looking stories. So what's your story? What's unique about your business? What announcement (news,) about you and your business can you pitch?

Sponsor Local

There are dozens of events and sports teams in your city that need your sponsorship. Consider trading services for sponsorship. I sponsor a national business networking group with web hosting and design.

Local SEO

- Look for local directories and submit.
- Participate in local forums.
- Use location keywords in your SEO. For example Toronto web design

Local Events

- Participate in local events.
- Join the local Chamber of Commerce.
- Attend local networking events and meetups
- Get vendor tables at local events
- Always display your website URL
 - Get banners
 - Business cards and other marketing materials
 - T-shirts and other promotional items
Consider hosting your own event

Having a heavy presence in your community is a great way to showcase you and your business and drive traffic to your website.

Social Media

On a scale of 1-5 rate the following on your social media.

1. I am on the big 3 social media websites
2. I post content regularly on social media
3. I engage on social media
4. I share others content on social media
5. My social media channels reflect my brand

Social Media allows you to promote you, your business and your interests. Use Social Media to get your name out there, whether a potential client interacts with your brand or not, having a social media presence generates name recognition. Social Media is an awesome way to market your business and drive traffic to your website. Social Media can be your biggest lead generator if done right. Social Media is a great place to showcase your expertise and promote your products and services.

Include social media profile icons are on the site.

Search engines love blogs; unique and frequent content is a great way to get ranked in search engines. Plan each post to promote your opt-ins and products and services. Mix in regular blog posts with evergreen blog posts (long, unique, and informative), controversial blog posts (take a stand and say what's on your mind) and trendy blog posts.

- Awesome content
- Easy to read posts (formatted with headings bullets, bold, etc.)
- Free resources, downloads, and printables
- Search Engine Optimize (SEO) all posts
- Branded image for each post

- Call to action on each post
- Share buttons on all posts

Get readers to interact and share your blog posts by including social media share buttons are on your website.

Monitor and track your blog using analytic tools such as Google Analytics. Measure how much traffic you get from each social media platform to your blog. Even go a step further and track conversions.

Share Your Content
As part of your social media strategy your blog editorial content calendar includes which social media platforms you plan to share each post on, when you will share and how often.

I recommend sharing on the date you publish, a week later and a month later. It's good to also create a plan on how you will share old blog posts.

Post all your blog posts on social media. Take time to schedule your posts to other social media platforms to get backlinks and build social currency and clout. Constantly use keyword rich hashtags.

In addition to posting your blog posts on social media platforms, use social bookmarking sites such as Delicious, StumbleUpon, Digg, and Reddit. Slowly bookmark all pages of your website not just blog posts to these sites. Just like with any other social media share others content too. Always post your blogs to your Google+ page to get instant Google cred.

In addition to sharing your blog posts, start guest blogging and commenting on others blogs.

Engagement in 15 Minutes A Day

On a daily basis check your feed to find posts that are either beneficial to your Awesome Nation or stand out on a personal level.

1. Share/Retweet/Pin

2. Like posts of people in your network, influencers, and clients

3. Comment/Reply

4. Respond to any communication via private message, or commenting on your posts.

5. Review posts in communities and groups to share, like, and comment on

6. Status updates if applicable

If you have a campaign or promotion running, 15 minutes of engagement can turn into an hour of engagement or more.

Use social media as an inspiration for posts on your blog. By observing what performs well and earns engagement, you can tailor your content.

Not only do you want to participate on social media, you want to be active and initiate conversation on social media too.

Get your copy of the Social Media Marketing: How to Master Engagement in 15 Minutes a Day.

Analysis

To effectively use any tool for marketing you have to see results. You can measure the success of Social Media if you outline clear goals and objectives. What are you trying to accomplish? What platforms are you using? What is the objective of each? What is the objective of each post? Social Media for business is possible. If you are:
- using Social Media for the right reasons,
- using the right platforms for your business,
- have measurable objectives in place,
- and are able to dedicate and commit time to Social Media
Only then you can make Social Media Successful for you!

Commitment

A lot of people say Social Media is a free form of advertising. Is it free? To successfully use Social Media, you must factor in your time. What is your commitment to social media marketing? Monthly, Weekly Daily? In 15 minutes a day? To make Social Media work for you, you need dedication, commitment and time.

Social media can be one of your biggest promoters and lead and sales generators if done correctly.

Download and complete the Social Media section in the Death of A Website Workbook and Planner.

Online Reputation Management

On a scale of 1-5 rate the following on your online reputation management.
1. I check my online reputation on a regular basis
2. I have secured my name on multiple social media websites
3. I provide excellent customer service
4. I encourage my clients to post reviews and write testimonials
5. I respond to any reviews and comments

An often neglected segment of online marketing is online reputation management (ORM). Your business needs to be conscious of its online reputation. You need to know what people are saying about you online.

The majority of people go online before they buy (#1 reason you should have a website) and if they see bad reviews they will turn to your competitor quickly.
Establish yourself as an authority. Niche down. Build credibility.
Secure your name everywhere.
Manage your Online Reputation on
- Search Engines
- Social Media
- Media / Press

Monitor your reputation. Lead the conversations about you in a positive manner. Ensure that whatever is said about you and your company is the truth, the good, the bad and the ugly. If you have negative mentions, figure out how to make it work for you. How can you do better?

Whether or not you have bad reviews, you need to know what people are saying about you online.

Negative Reviews = lost business

1. Try to resolve issue

2. Respond professionally - provide a solution

3. Commit publicly - reply directly under review with a positive comment

4. Respond ASAP

5. Empathize

Never write fake reviews.

Never trade insults. Be professional.

Good reviews = happy clients = more business

Influence new reviews, and increase positive reviews by ensuring everyone you encounter has an exceptional experience.
- Employees
- Vendors
- Clients
- Prospects
Encourage client reviews and industry reviews.
Promote positive reviews.

Track, address and repair.

Track and monitor what is being said about you online. Clients, prospects, competitors and suppliers are online - a bad reputation can spread fast.

Protect your business reputation and integrity by tracking your online presence.
- Search engine search
- Social media search
- Review websites
Use Google alerts and a feed reader to monitor what is being said about you.

Address the issue
Deal with issues before they become a problem for your business.
Read online reviews, respond - thank for positive reviews and deal swiftly with any complaints.

Damage Repair
- Contact website / social media where you have a bad review.
- Encourage honest customer reviews
- Consider hiring a reputation management firm
- Do not threaten legal action. It's not as easy or logical as it seems. Most reviewers are protected by rights

You can take preventative action by treating your clients and potential clients the way you wanted to be treated.
Always encourage existing clients to post honest reviews. Give incentives to encourage clients to leave reviews.

Other ways to keep a pristine reputation is by creating mega value content, using SEO and social media effectively. Send out positive press releases on a regular basis. And be accessible. You can nip dissatisfaction in the bud by taking client surveys as well.

Don't neglect your online reputation.

Email

On a scale of 1-5 rate the following on your website.
1. Use email signature
2. Send out updates to customers using email
3. Try to get all customers addresses
4. I regularly send out an Ezine (Newsletter)
5. I use email to update customers about Promotions

Phase 1 - Capture Leads
Phase one of email marketing is covered in the last chapter: Capturing Leads. Be sure to provide many opportunities to generate leads.

Phase 2 - Email Marketing is Branding
Use your email to build brand recognition by personalizing and customizing your email. Use email to not only build trust but also recognition.
- Use a professional email address @yourbusiness.com
- Make it more personal by using your real name.
- Create a branded email template, include your logo.
- Always include an email signature with links and buttons to your website and social media.
- A great way to promote your products and services is to include an image in your signature.

It is an effective way to keep top of mind of your prospects and turn your clients into frequent buyers.

Phase 3 - Respect Permission Based Marketing

When people sign up for your opt-in or newsletter they are giving you permission to email them. Ensure you get permission. Don't just send out email to random people. It feels like an invasion of privacy. Allow people to unsubscribe. Use professional email service providers such as MailChimp or Aweber or ConvertKit to mange your email and send campaigns.

Phase 4 - Professional Email

Whether sending a regular email to prospects, customers, vendors, or a campaign; be professional. Don't use free email providers for your business email.

Communicate effectively with email. Emails should be brief and focused - in ten seconds the reader should know what it's about. Be concise and use short sentences and bullet points. Use a meaningful subject line and make sure content is relevant to your receiver. Be careful of image and attachment size and broken links.

You don't have to be tied to your email screen all day. You can schedule your email activities to once a day.

Phase 5 - Customer Service

Email is a great way to stay in touch and follow up. Respond promptly to inquiries and clients.

Your email can be an effective customer service tool. Create a list of Frequently Asked Questions (FAQ) with responses so when a customer asks a question you can respond quickly and efficiently.

Phase 6 - Marketing and Selling

Use your email to nurture leads and turn them into sales. Email is the prefect tool to get people to know, like and trust you.

To expertly manage your email create lists and segments. Divide your lists into clients and prospects. Further segment clients into A list and top clients and segment prospects by interest.

Always have a 7-12 email autoresponder ready for options and problems. Develop email campaigns around every opt-in and every purchase, and every new product/service. Provide a call to action in every email. It can be as simple as asking for a reply to encourage engagement. Email is also a great way to get feedback. Consider split testing subject lines and email content. Also consider sending surveys to clients and prospects. Track open and and click through rates.

Email can be a very effective promotional tool. Don't discount supping up regular emails. And remember the money is in the list.

Advertising

On a scale of 1-5 rate the following on your website.
1. I advertise now or plan to in the next 12 months.
2. I have an advertising budget.
3. I have an advertising plan.
4. I have air plan to use social media advertising.

5. I have reviewed advertising options.

Before embarking on an advertising campaign, create a plan.

1. Objective - what do you want to accomplish?

2. Call to Action - what do you want people to do?

3. Budget - What's your budget?

4. Create the ad

5. Metrics - Did it work? Did you achieve your objective?

You have options when using online advertising:

Display Ads - Google AdSense which is paid per click (PPC), you pay when people click on the links

Pay for product reviews

Do giveaways on your website and partner with others

Sponsorship - sponsor blog posts, social media, podcasts and videos (Sponsored by...)

Affiliate Marketing - pay others to promote you. You provide marketing collateral such as banners, product images and sales copy to affiliates.

Classified Ads - use free and paid services to get your business, products and services

Email Ads - you can get others to advertise you in their emails by sponsorship or pay-per-click

Social Media Ads - It can be an affordable way to reach a larger targeted audience. It's easy to track and analyize.

Action Plan

Get Found
Plan and implement a website submission schedule.
Revise all your marketing collateral to include your website.

Get Local
Revise your SEO to include local keywords if applicable.
Make a schedule list of local events you want to attend, participate or sponsor.

Social Media Marketing
Optimize your website for social media.
Monitor and track social media
Practice 15 minutes of social media a day. **Get the Social Media Marketing: How to Master Engagement in 15 Minutes a Day.**

Rank social media in order of importance.
Decide where you will focus your engagement and marketing.
Consider the 80/20 rule.

How often do you engage on social media a week?

Email Marketing
Clean up your email lists.
- Remove people that don't open

- Segment based on clients, prospects etc.

Create your email templates / FAQ.

Download email etiquette.

Review your business email and email campaigns:
- Is it branded?
- Is it professional?

Create an autoresponder around each offer, product, service, and opt-in.

Advertising

Download and complete the Advertising section in the Death of A Website Workbook and Planner.
#

Action Plan

Chapter Eight
Life Support

Optimization, Maintenance and Metrics

Hooray! It turns out you haven't killed your website yet. In addition to design, branding and awesome content and offers, and marketing - optimizing, maintaining and tracking your website success will keep your website alive. Don't commit the neglect offence.

Optimizing Your Website

Speed

On a scale of 1-5 rate the following on your website.
1. I check my site regularly for speed
2. I have accessed my site using different web browsers
3. I have accessed my site using different computers
4. I optimize images
5. I use page caching on my website

Slow loading websites don't pass the 3-second rule and Google takes site speed into account in their search ranking.

To speed up your website the number one thing you do is design for speed.

1. When you design your site think of page size in terms of bytes, the bigger the slower the website

2. Optimize your images. You may be tempted to load images directly from your smartphone but take the time to make them smaller and faster to load. Most themes will come with a pre-

set blog image size. Resize your images to take advantage of your theme.

3. Don't reference images from other sites - copy them and then upload. When a website fetches an image from another website it over extends load time. Also adhere to copyright laws and give credit for images.

4. Don't use word processing to create HTML, word processors such as Microsoft Office add their own mark-up that can increase a page size

5. Compress images. Use programs like smushit to compress images.

6. Minimize code such as HTML, JavaScript, CSS (Don't forget to remove any unused CSS) to speed up loading and save bytes.

7. Remove spam comments from your website.

8. Remove unnecessary white space, line breaks and indents.

9. Most CMS websites run on PHP and a database connection. Use page caching to turn dynamic pages into static pages, reducing the number of requests to the web server.

10.Before you use Iframes note that it slows down the page loading.

Slow load time increases abandonment rate. Remember the 3-second rule applies to page loads. Make your visitors and search engines happy with a quick website.

Broken Links

On a scale of 1-5 rate the following on your website.

1. I regularly check for broken links
2. I fix broken links immediately
3. I use 301 Redirect when I move pages
4. I have a branded 404-error message page
5. I review the stats and turn "Not Found Pages" into content creation opportunities

BAD LINKS SUCK! No one wants to have broken links on their website. The more links you have both external and internal the more you should be checking. No one wants to have broken links on their website. Sometimes a visitor will come to your website based on a link that does not exist.
Broken links happen:
- External website page is removed or renamed
- Misspelling in the link
- Mistake when posting link
- Change in file name or structure

Sometimes a visitor will come to your site based on a link that does not exist. That is when you use error messages to your benefit and brand your 404 and 403 pages.

When you have too many broken links, visitors get frustrated and won't return. Bad links create a bad user experience. It looks like you don't care about your site - NEGLECT - and you lose SEO status when search engines can't find a page and stops search engines from completely indexing your site - DEVALUES SEO.

Be vigilant for external links.
Heal Your Website - Fix Broken Links

I recommend checking for broken links on a monthly basis. The more links you have both external and internal the more you should be checking. Always check links after major upgrades and updates.

Review Google Webmaster Tools for crawl errors and Google Analytics to find bad links. Analyze if it's a typo or if the page moved and fix the links.

Include a branded 404-error page (standard HTTP response that indicates the requested URL does not exist) for internal errors and use 301 Redirect when you move pages.

Bad Links leave a bad taste and visitors will leave, never to return.

Error Message

On a scale of 1-5 rate the following on your website.
1. I have created customized error messages
2. I have branded error messages
3. I read the stats for the error messages
4. I fix the problems that cause error messages
5. Optimize error page to redirect to internal links FAQ Page or opt-in

In addition to bad links, you can get an error message due to coding (see validation), out-dated plugin, or out-dated CMS. Be sure to keep plugins and WordPress updated as well as make note of error messages to discuss with your web designer.

When people come to your site no one wants to see an error message. But you can use error messages to your benefit. Creating a customized error message that leads visitors to where you want to go or capture information such as email for an email list.

Every month check for error messages and fix them. Sometimes a visitor will type in the wrong address and that is why they get an error. See what they were trying to find and capitalize on it. For example they typed in www.awesomebizonline.com/taxes. I don't have that page, but I can create it or use taxes as a keyword for my website.

Be diligent about fixing and anticipating errors. You can't prepare for every issue so use error messages to your advantage.

Website Maintenance

On a scale of 1-5 rate the following on your website.
1. I backup my website on a regular basis
2. I manage comments
3. I regularly update the theme
4. I regularly update plugins
5. I regularly update WordPress

Website Maintenance is a very important to running a successful and healthy website.

Unless you are tech savvy, it's useful to have at least someone to help you with any backend issues. While creating content is at the heart of online marketing, technical support is necessary to improve the performance of your websites and ensure everything works right.

Make sure your website is configured correctly to ensure it has a strong foundation.

It's important to review your website maintenance on a monthly basis (**Website Maintenance Worksheet included in Death of A Website Workbook and Planner**)

Keep your software up-to-date and secure. This means using the latest version of your software (i.e., WordPress) and taking other security measures. For example, not using "admin" for your administrator's username. One of the many reasons to use WordPress is because it has free regular software updates for security and feature enhancements.

Even though WordPress is awesome, you do need additional tools for optimal functionality such as analytics, social media sharing and others to run your website. Configuring your website for plugins also includes choosing the best plugins for these services.

Keep your plugins updated Just like your WordPress software; you need to keep the plugins you've installed up to date as well. By keeping compatible with the latest WordPress update you avoid security breaches and a broken website.

Reduce plugins. While plug-ins are great for solving problems, they take time to load, hinder performance and could add security vulnerabilities. Only have installed plugins that are essential to running your website, remove any unused plugins.

On a regular basis clean out and optimize your blog's database.

Maintain your blog comments regularly. Clear out any spam that's been caught by your spam filter and don't miss replying to any visitors that have replied to your blog posts.

SEO Analysis and Update

You want to regularly analyze and update:
- Browser Titles
- Meta Data
- Keywords

Use tools such as Google Analytics to analyze your site. It is a free analysis tool that helps you track visitors, referring sites, search engines, keywords used, and much more.

Remember to Backup!

This is without a doubt something that's neglected by most website owners. They don't realize that if something happened and their website goes down (as rare that it happens) that they have nothing backed up. The best way to backup is to use a backup plugin such as Vaultpress or Backup Buddy. Plugins like these can be installed and setup, so backups are created automatically and saved to your hosting server, cloud server or hard drive for a fee.

In addition to being a good practice in case you have a technical problems, having a full backup allows you to move your site at any time.

Create a Web Maintenance Plan that outlines how often you need to update your website, who will maintain and update the website.

1. Update WordPress

2. Update plugins and revise unused plugins

3. Update theme

4. Manage comments

5. Back up website on a regular basis (daily, weekly, monthly)

6. Update content

7. Check for broken links

8. Review and update SEO

Download Free Web Maintenance Report

Measure Your Website Metrics

On a scale of 1-5 rate the following on your website
1. I check my stats regularly
2. I review traffic on a regular basis
3. I know the top referring sites
4. Track marketing efforts
5. Have a tracking software on my website such as Google analytics

What's the point of having a website if it just sits there and does nothing? How do you know if it is doing something, anything? How do you know your website is working? Besides seeing actual sales - money in hand, you can track and monitor your website and overall online marketing success.

Sadly, many business owners don't have a single clue if their website is effective. Not only that, but they don't know which pages are getting viewed, which ones are useless, and how much time visitors are actually hanging around their website.

Master analytics, learn to how to read and understand reports. Analytics is invaluable to your websites growth and success. Website metrics is your guide to understanding what's working and what's not working, how you can improve and give readers what they want.

Set Goals and Targets
- Generate clients, traffic and leads
- Track conversion
- Know where visitors come from
- Know what they do on the site and learn to direct them where you want them to do, why do they leave, when do they leave?
- What do you want them to do before they leave?

Track and Monitor Your Website. Whether you call it metrics, key performance indicators (KPI), analytics, etc. you should be doing it on a consistent basis. Your level of monitoring is in conjunction with how quickly you can react. Checking your stats daily means you are able to capitalize on the results immediately.

The first part of your metrics is to gauge your ability to **Attract Visitors / Drive Traffic.**
Using Google Analytics or another tracking tool you can track visitors, unique visitors, and where they go on your website. Is the number of page views where you want it to be? So you need to improve SEO keyword ranking and increase inbound

links. (Are you coming up with the right keywords if at all and how many relevant sites link to you?)

Traffic - Knowing which website pages receive the highest number of views can help you determine the type of content to post.

Visitors - Track visitors, unique visitors, where they come from and what sections they go to.

Referral Tracking - Know who sends traffic your way. This enables you to see which websites most refer readers to your website. Learn if your SEO efforts are working, and what social media sites send the most traffic. Out of all the stats, this one lets you know if your online marketing is working and what methods are worth investing your time in.

Do you know where is traffic coming from?
- Direct (a direct link to your website)
- Referral (link from another website)
- Organic (referred by search engine)
- Social media

Content Marketing - Page views show the number of times your blog has been viewed over a specific period of time. This number includes new visitors and returning readers alike. You can track per day & per month (& versus prior period) of specific pages. Also review downloads, clicks on links, RSS signups, email signups, and where readers exit.

SEO - Find out which keyword searches lead readers to your website. Create content around popular keyword searches to your website. Also, use your website to answer search questions.

Search Engine Optimize your website with relevant keywords and inbound links to improve your keyword ranking.

While attracting visitors to your website build brand awareness and recognition with consistency. By reviewing your metrics and website on a regular basis enables you to remain consistent.

The next part of your website objective is to **Capture Leads.** Offering opportunities to engage on your website is a big part of this objective.
- Create a Community (time spent/bounce rate)
- Build Your List (subscribers)
- Create Engagement (comments)
- Content marketing (click on links, opt-ins, RSS signups, average pages per visit, and downloads)

Time Spent on Website - See how much time people are spending on your website when they visit. If your bounce rate is high and people are not spending time on your website, it's time to review why.

Bounce Rate - A low bounce rate means that people are spending time on your site and reading several posts when they visit.

Engagement - Find out about social media shares and social media engagement in your analysis. Review blog comments, shares, likes and comments on social media.

How many people are visiting your website from social media and are they engaging on your website? Learn which blog posts do well on social media. Use Google Analytics in conjunction with Bitly, Buffer, Hootsuite or other reporting tools and the social media platform analytics to track and monitor your social media success.

Every month you should review your website content to ensure its still relevant, useful and shareable.

You should have a process for reviewing and updating your site. This helps with keeping you fresh in the eyes of Google.

The last part of your website objective is to **Make Sales**.

Does your website allow people to buy and does it have a sales funnel to turn leads into sales?
You want to look at the conversion from visitor to leads (opt-in / subscription) to clients (how you sell using your mailing list) as well as visitor to clients (how you sell on your website).

Track links and split tests on landing and sales page to see which page is best. It seems like a lot of work, but once you develop a system based on results it will make the whole process easier.

After you get your leads and sales numbers you also want to review your expenses (cost of running your website) to get your return on investment as well as your sales cycle (how to reduce the length of time to purchase), reduce customer service requests and any returns.

Learn more about your return on investment (ROI – time and money) as well as which website pages bring the most traffic, engagement, and conversion.

Most analytics programs allow you to specify a certain period of time to display a graph charting the growth of your blog. This way, you can review the past three months, the past year, or the growth of your website since its beginning.

Tracking is crucial, especially when using content marketing. You want to keep track of where people are coming from and what messages are resonating and making people take action.

Don't forget to evaluate.
Every month and quarter see if you have achieved the goals you set out for yourself. Set new goals and benchmarks. Test and adjust strategy as needed.

Feedback

Ask at least 5 people to review your website. Ask them the following questions.

1. Do you instantly know what the website is about?
2. Is there anything confusing?
3. Can you easily find the newsletter signup, sales page?
4. Is the website cluttered?
5. Do you have any other feedback?

An often neglected aspect of metrics is to just ask. Ask your visitors and clients for feedback.

Find out from your prospects, subscribers and clients what products and services they want, what they think of your communication, and customer service. How do they find using your website? (Complete the Website Feedback Questionnaire)

Don't just ask people you know for feedback, take advantage of social media. Social Media Groups are a great way to get feedback from validated prospects.

Solicit feedback by providing multiple ways for clients and prospects to contact you on your website and social media profiles.

Action Plan

At the beginning of this book, we asked you what are your objectives. Now it is time to rate your objectives. Are you accomplishing what you set out to do?

One way for you to meet your objectives is to optimize, maintain, track and analyze your website on a frequent consistent basis.

Optimize your website - check for speed, broken links and 404 errors.
Download our free guide to web maintenance and create your web maintenance plan now. Develop a maintenance program now or hire Awesome Biz Online to manage it for you.

Review your website analytics and update your website accordingly to increase traffic (attract visitors), increase leads

Action Plan

and increase sales. Review your website content to ensure its still relevant, useful and shareable monthly.

You should have a process for reviewing and updating your site. This helps with keeping you fresh in the eyes of Google.

Chapter Nine
Don't Be The Villain

You are the villain in this crime when you put your needs above the needs of your clients and visitors of your website.

Create Your Action Plan

Congratulations you have not killed your website. Now it's time to breath new life by creating an action plan.

1. Make a list of your website issues that need to be fixed. What is the number one improvement you can do right now to make your website better?

2. Next, prioritize your list based on the sales funnel.
Step 1 - Attract Visitors
Step 2 - Qualified Leads
Step 3 - Sales
Step 4 - Optimize and Maintain

3. Once you have prioritized your website improvements for a better money making website, create an action plan with action steps. For each issue create your first action steps and next action steps to fix the issue.

4. Set Deadlines. For each issue add a completion date / due date. Set realistic dates. Don't sabotage yourself and your website by not allowing enough time to resolve each issue properly.

5. Delegate. If you can get someone with more expertise than you to get the job done, do it. Outsourcing or hiring experts is a great way to bring your website to the next level faster.

You can hire a web designer to make improvements on your website, hire a blogger for content, or get a SEO expert to optimize your website.

Contact Awesome Biz Online for a free consultation.

6. Implement Improvements. Act now. Make website improvements for an awesome website. Don't hesitate. Start.

7. Make a commitment to do one thing every day to convert your website into a cash machine.

THANK-YOU

HOPE YOU ENJOYED READING
Death of A Website:
Don't Make These 7 Killer Website Mistakes

**PLEASE LEAVE A REVIEW WHERE YOU
PURCHASED THE BOOK**

The exercises in this book can be found in the **Death of A
Website Death of A Website Workbook and Planner.**

**DOWNLOAD YOUR COPY OF THE 76 PAGE
Death of A Website Death of A Website Workbook
and Planner**
http://dwainiagrey.me/blogging-workbook-download/

GET YOUR FREE BLOGGING BONUSES!
http://dwainiagrey.me/death-of-a-website-bonuses/

ALSO LOOK OUT FOR
*Authentic Marketing – The Three E's of Online Marketing:
Ethical, Effortless, Engaging*

Connect with Dwainia Grey on
LinkedIn, Google+, Facebook, Twitter, Pinterest and
Instagram
dwainiagrey.me

BONUS

Join the **Empowerpreneur League** Facebook Group to network with others for support, feedback, brainstorming, growth and tips. This group is 100% Free and made up of Empowerpreneurs across the world.
http://bit.ly/empowerpreneur-league

You can also join us on LinkedIn.
http://bit.ly/empowerpreneur-marketing

BE SURE TO GRAB YOUR COPIES

- Social Media Marketing: How to Master Engagement in 15 Minutes a Day

- Social Media Marketing: How to Master Engagement in 15 Minutes a Day Workbook and Planner and Planner-

- Facebook Media Marketing

- Google+ Death of A Website Workbook and Planner and Planner -

- LinkedIn Death of A Website Workbook and Planner and Planner -

- Twitter Death of A Website Workbook and Planner and Planner -

- Pinterest Death of A Website Workbook and Planner and Planner -

- Instagram Death of A Website Workbook and Planner and Planner -

www.ingramcontent.com/pod-product-compliance
Lightning Source LLC
Chambersburg PA
CBHW060606200326
41521CB00007B/677